Queen Victoria's
SKETCHBOOK

Queen Victoria's
SKETCHBOOK

MARINA WARNER

Crown Publishers Inc. New York

First published by Macmillan London Ltd in England, 1979

Queen Victoria's Sketches copyright © Her Majesty
   Queen Elizabeth II 1979
Text copyright © Marina Warner 1979
Design copyright © Macmillan London Limited 1979

The publishers thank Her Majesty Queen Elizabeth II for her
gracious permission to reproduce the portrait of Princess
Victoria by Richard Westall, R.A., on page 22; and H.R.H.
The Duke of Kent for his kind permission to reproduce the
portrait of Prince Albert by Queen Victoria on page 91 and on
the jacket.

Design by Robert Updegraff

Printed in Great Britain

Library of Congress Cataloging in Publication Data
   Victoria, Queen of Great Britain, 1819–1901.
   Queen Victoria's sketchbook.
   1. Victoria, Queen of Great Britain, 1819–1901.
   I. Warner, Marina, 1946–   II. Title.
   NC242.V52A4 1979   741.9′42   79-13218

   ISBN 0-517-53936-5

Contents

Acknowledgements

The publishers and I most gratefully acknowledge the permission of Her Majesty The Queen to sift the many sketchbooks of Queen Victoria in the Royal Collection, and to match sketches with entries in Queen Victoria's Journal.

I owe an enormous debt of gratitude to Sir Robin Mackworth-Young, K.C.V.O., the Royal Librarian, to Jane Roberts, Curator of the Print Room, and to the Deputy Curator, Charlotte Miller. Everyone in the Royal Archives was helpfulness itself: my deepest thanks go to Jane Langton, M.V.O., Elizabeth Cuthbert, Sheila de Bellaigue and Frances Dimond. The House Governor at Osborne kindly allowed me to visit the Queen's apartments, and I am indebted to Edward Sibbick for his encyclopaedic information on the house and its collection.

Lady Longford gave me invaluable advice on the finished manuscript; Daphne Bennett also was most generous with her comments; Dr Roy Foster, besides helping me throughout with bibliographic references, also read the manuscript.

Elizabeth Johnston's research for the Royal Performance exhibition at Windsor in 1977 provided the first inspiration for this book, and later she gave me her enthusiastic support. Victoria Moger helped me greatly by researching aspects of Victoria's theatre-going, and child-bearing and rearing in her day. Bernard Nevill invited me to read Queen Alexandra's bound volumes of *The Graphic* magazine, and Christopher Wood helped me place Victoria's watercolours in the context of their day. My sister Laura Warner's work on Italian opera was an illumination.

My special thanks go also to all who helped me while I was writing by looking after my son Conrad. It is to him that I dedicate this book.

Marina Warner
London, 1979

Introduction

In 1845 the Danseuses Viennoises danced before the Queen in her own theatre — Her Majesty's in the Haymarket — in the Pas des Moissoneurs, from the ballet Käya, ou l'Amour Voyageur.

In sketches such as this Victoria expressed her gaiety and her tremendous love of life.

Queen Victoria personified to an uncanny degree the values of the era that is justly called after her. Over the sixty-three years of her reign she was the cynosure of all eyes, and her influence governed the direction, ambition and ideals of the subjects under her. In the first sense of the word, she was the cliché of her age, the cast from which it took its unique imprint. She was thrifty, but capable of largesse; she was affectionate, even passionate, but rarely unbridled and never wanton; she was a devoted mother, but had decided ideas about the duties of children. The deadliest sin in her view was sloth, and the parable most suited to her nature and the character of her times is that of the talents, with its stern warning that native gifts should never lie buried and unused.

But Victoria was not puritanical, and she made her industry serve her pleasure. She kept, with infectious enthusiasm, a journal of her life from 1832 until her death in 1901; her voluminous correspondence to friends, relations, and later to her children when they married and left home, bubbles over with news, plans, hints and solicitude. She tackled with gritty dedication the heaps of despatches in the boxes sent by her ministers; she received guests continually; she played the piano and sang; and in between, she painted.

For Queen Victoria was an artist. The first date on a small sketchbook in the Royal Collection is 1827, the last, inscribed in a wobbly hand on a loose sheet of paper, is 1890. There are over fifty of her albums and sketchbooks, and only very few of the drawings and watercolours which fill them have been reproduced before. She has been, until now, an unknown example of a marvellous and extinct breed: the Victorian amateur watercolourist.

Victoria drew and painted to chronicle her daily life. She was an amateur not in the later pejorative sense of Sunday painter, but because she had no higher aim than to seize the fugitive moment. She very seldom created a picture from imagination, and the contemporary Pre-Raphaelite movement never touched her. She certainly had a gift, particularly for a quick, lively likeness of one of her children or her friends, but she made no claims to profound portraiture. If art had been her first vocation, she would have failed; because it was a hobby amongst many, she distinguished herself.

Apart from their intrinsic charm Queen Victoria's paintings and drawings have a historical importance. She was the monarch who ruled during the epoch of which we are the direct heirs, as beneficiaries and as victims, and her art forms a distant yet audible accompaniment to the policies that were carried out under her rule. Through her sketches of genre scenes and picturesque peasantry we see the age's bafflement at the reality of poverty. Her tender portraits of her children announce the clear ascendancy of the family as an institution to be given all protection — the Victorians were the first to legislate for the rights of married women and children. Her watercolours of Germany reveal the love and fascination she felt for her mother and her husband's country, and her loyalty to Albert's conception of his homeland was reflected in the conduct of foreign policy. Her attraction to exoticism, dark-eyed and dusky, is part of the dream that took the English to Africa, India and all points faraway.

Victoria was too practical to adopt the confessional tone, too dedicated to self-improvement to make an exhibition of herself. Yet she also had a prodigal capacity for self-revelation. Her drawings and her paintings are guileless, as she was. Their strength is her strength: impetuosity, quick decisiveness, spontaneity, loyalty to her own perception, obstinacy in her likes and dislikes, readiness to admire, to enjoy and to praise.

ONE

Kensington Palace

In 1865, when Queen Victoria was a widow of forty-six, the Mock Turtle sighed to Alice that he had only taken 'the regular course' of lessons. 'What was that?' Alice asked. The curriculum the Gryphon and the Mock Turtle then described would not have been unrecognizable to the Queen of England. It resembled, in almost all particulars, the education she received at Kensington Palace from her early childhood to her accession at the age of eighteen in 1837. 'Reeling and Writhing, of course', said the Mock Turtle. In later years Victoria admitted in a memoir: 'I was not fond of learning as a little child — and baffled every attempt to teach me my letters up to 5 years old — when I consented to learn them by their being written down before me.'

'And then the different branches of Arithmetic', proceeded the Turtle. Louise Lehzen, Victoria's governess, must have taught her charge the rudiments of mathematics; but in the diary Victoria kept from 1832 until her death there is no record that any branch of arithmetic held any appeal for her.

Louise Lehzen, created a Hanoverian baroness by King George IV in 1826, was the most important influence on Victoria's childhood. She became devoted to the Princess with maternal and possessive intensity.

'What else had you to learn?' asked Alice, perhaps equally impatient to pass on to other subjects. 'Well, there was Mystery . . . ancient and modern.' History was one of Victoria's delights. Guided principally by her mother's brother, King Leopold of the Belgians, Victoria read widely in memoirs and manuals, from Sully to the French Academician Gaillard's history of Franco-Spanish tensions. But, as she explained to Uncle Leopold: 'The history of my own country is one of my first duties.'

Victoria's schooling in history was intense, but not systematic. Lehzen would read aloud to the little Princess morning and night while her hair was being brushed by her maid, so that she should always employ her time profitably and also learn not to chatter in front of domestics. The governess, daughter of a Lutheran pastor, was strict but not joyless: her taste, fortunately for Victoria, was lighter than that of Uncle Leopold. She began by reading stories to the small girl, and history was served later in the delectable form

A small red leather sketchpad with horizontal pages was given to Princess Victoria by Lehzen in 1827, when she was eight years old. In it she drew this picture of herself, with her hair fresh out of screwpapers.

an race horse.

One of Victoria's earliest drawings from her first sketchbook, before Richard Westall's tuition had begun to tell.

of Walter Scott's writings — exciting and romantic, certainly, but also deeply instructive of the historical and social forces that toss all individuals, be they queens or commoners. It was Lehzen who defended Victoria's pleasure in reading contemporary travels and memoirs. On the diary of the famous actress Fanny Kemble, Victoria commented: 'There are some fine feelings and descriptions . . . but upon the whole it is pertly and sometimes *even* vulgarly written.'

In *Alice*, to the Mock Turtle's account the Gryphon adds that he had been taught 'Laughing and Grief'. Victoria learned no Greek, and when, on a visit to Oxford in 1832, she was shown Queen Elizabeth I's Latin exercise book, she was awed. 'She was of my age (13)', she wrote in her diary. But when the Mock Turtle had counted off on his flappers Mystery and Seaography, he came to the accomplishment included in the 'regular course' of all Victorian children of gentle birth. 'Then Drawling', he said. 'The Drawlingmaster was an old conger-eel, that used to come once a week: *he* taught us Drawling, Stretching, and Fainting in Coils.'

In 1827, when Victoria was eight years old, she received her first drawing lesson from Richard Westall, R.A. From then on until his death nine years later, he called at Kensington Palace twice a week to give her hour-long lessons. But Mr Westall, of whom we shall hear more later, was only one of a team of visiting instructors in the polite arts. There was Madame Bourdin, Victoria's dancing teacher; Mrs Anderson, her music and singing mistress; John Sale, impresario and organist at St Margaret's, Westminster, who taught her piano; and others for French, German and Italian, languages being considered an essential part of her education. Her chief tutor was the Very Rev. George Davys, Dean of Chester, who was responsible for her education as a whole and for her religious instruction. He came for two hours most mornings, but sometimes, Victoria records ruefully, for the whole day. The Duchess of Northumberland was her official governess, ranking above Lehzen, though Lehzen retained her considerable influence over Victoria right up to the painful time when first Lord Melbourne, and later Prince Albert, replaced her in the young Queen's strong affections.

It was Lehzen who taught Victoria to keep a meticulous account of her daily schedule. Her first Journal opens with the inscription, written in sepia ink in a vigorous, sloping and angular hand: 'This book Mama gave me, that I might write the journal of my journey to Wales in it. — Victoria, Kensington Palace, July 31'. But when such refreshing material as a journey was lacking, the diary has a sad, clock-punching look: 'I awoke at 7 and got up at $\frac{1}{2}$ past 7. At $\frac{1}{2}$ past 8 we breakfasted. At $\frac{1}{2}$ past 9 came the Dean till 11. At $\frac{1}{2}$ past 12 we lunched . . . At $\frac{1}{2}$ past 2 came Mr Westall till $\frac{1}{2}$ past 3 . . . '

Westall came to teach the Princess drawing and sketching (but not painting in oils). She reports sometimes that he was pleased with her work, and that she admired him; she saw 'some great beauties by Westall, my master' at Downton Castle, near Shrewsbury (where they still are). But only after his death in 1836 did Victoria pay him generous, emotional tribute, and then she was moved more by pity for his financial state than by ardour for a master who had truly

Lehzen, the Princess's first regularly available sitter, inspired portraits which reveal that assurance of line and spontaneity of approach which remained Victoria's strongest artistic qualities.

14

a sketch
from nature
2 V.f. R.P. charac? L.
1833.

16

inspired her. 'He was a very indulgent, patient, agreeable master, and a very worthy man . . . I have had every reason to be satisfied with him; he was very gentlemanly in his manners and extremely punctual and exact in everything he did.'

Richard Westall came from artistic stock. His father William was a melancholy man, who travelled with the explorer Matthew Flinders on his voyage to the Pacific, and provided the beautiful, grand illustrations of the natives, flora and fauna of Australia for the expedition's report to the Admiralty. Richard was apprenticed to a silver engraver, and later studied at the Royal Academy schools. He began as a portrait painter, but in the first quarter of the century he concentrated on illustrating editions of the poets. The cleanly chiselled lines of the engraver survived in all his later draughtsmanship. The study drawings he produced for his pupil to copy are distinguished by an exquisite delicacy of contour, set down upon the paper with a lightness and assurance that belies his age and his ill-health.

Though Westall could never be considered first rate, his drawings echo those of the greatest of his older contemporaries, John Flaxman, William Blake and Henry Fuseli. He shares with them a firmness of outline, and a leaning towards exaggerated facial expressions — knitted brows, rapt eyes, and dramatic gestures contained within a formal style, expressed with none of the impressionism of the later romantics. But the imagination and energy of Blake or Fuseli is entirely missing. Though in later years Westall adapted himself successfully to the needs of the times, abandoning the classics for the new authors, illustrating Goethe's *Faust*, Byron's *Don Juan* and Walter Scott's poems, he remained a peaceable artist, strikingly skilful but lacking in fire.

Princess Victoria was his first and only pupil. She had an artistic talent inherited from both sides of her family. Her grandfather George III was a collector of genius but also an accomplished draughtsman, as were his daughters, Augusta Sophia and Elizabeth. On the Coburg side, the Duchess of

Lehzen encouraged Victoria to make genealogical tables of the English sovereigns. It was when the young Princess saw her own name added to the bottom of the tree that she realized how close she was to the throne.

17

Kent had herself painted a *trompe-l'oeil* conservatory at the Rosenau in Coburg, her home before her first marriage. This talent Westall undoubtedly fostered with patient attention and some generosity.

Victoria copied Westall's drawings, of horses, of hands, of eyes. His lessons stuck: she always relied on her linear technique and was adept at catching the expression in a subject's eyes, at setting down the movement of a pony, or using a hand gesture to capture mood. Westall was also fond of genre painting, and he did a number of finished studies for Victoria — of a peasant girl drawing water at a well, a mother teaching her child, a begging urchin given alms by a mother holding her baby — and thus he instilled in her a

On her mother's birthday, 17 August, Victoria often presented her with a highly finished watercolour copied from her drawing master Richard Westall. These Tyrolese peasants with their prettily coloured local costume show his influence clearly.

This careful study of the horse Shrewsbury was also copied from Westall as a present for Mama.

Shrewsbury.

Victoria.
c Aug: 17th 1830.

conventional, picturesque approach to scenes of ordinary life about her, often spoiled by pretty-pretty colouring. She never succeeded in shaking off this tradition and achieving a more committed realism. But through his attachment to scenes of humble life, Westall taught the Princess to use her eyes. Her observation of details of dress, for instance, is strong in all her work.

On New Year's Day and on the birthday of 'Mama', Victoria several times made a fair copy of one of Westall's compositions as a present for her. For a girl in her teens, she was very sure with her pencil and her brush, but it is clear that her application soon waned, for if there are two figures in

Westall, there is usually only one that bears the legend, 'P.V. *del*. K.P.' — Princess Victoria *delineavit* Kensington Palace. Sometimes she made copies for charity; some of these survive, adding lustre to Victoria's reputation in places as far flung as the University of Auckland, New Zealand, while the composition's originator, Westall, is almost forgotten. One drawing was presented by Victoria to the United States Embassy in exchange for Fenimore Cooper's autograph.

An artist's career was even more precarious in the early decades of the nineteenth century than it is now, and Westall was in great straits. He was supporting a blind sister on his meagre income, and some dabbling in picture-dealing had gone awry. But he refused to accept payment for the lessons he gave the future Queen, though his sister received help from the Duchess of Kent. To Victoria, who was tender-hearted towards others' misfortunes, his penury was very bitter. 'He died in the *greatest* state of *pecuniary* distress', she wrote. 'This killed him. It *grieves* and *pains* me beyond measure that I could not alleviate his sufferings.' He told her mother that he was dying of a broken heart. 'Oh! this is sad, very very sad! to think that one whom I saw so often, knew so well, and who was so ready to oblige me, should *die* in want and overwhelmed by grief is grievous indeed!' In one of the very few passages of her diary as a Princess that betrays her knowledge of the great fortune awaiting her, Victoria continued: 'I could no more, as I had hoped, at a future time, make him comfortable and render his old days cheerful and without those worldly cares which . . . have brought him to the grave in a peculiarly distressing manner.' Westall left a letter for the Duchess of Kent, Victoria's mother, to be opened after his death. In it he begged her to settle £100 a year on his sister. This the Duchess of Kent naturally did, though the household at Kensington Palace was itself beset by all sorts of financial problems, caused partly by King William IV's dislike of his sister-in-law, and partly by the unscrupulousness and mismanagement of the Comptroller of the Duchess of Kent's household, the opportunist Sir John Conroy.

Westall's Hagar and Ishmael in the Desert *was exhibited at the Royal Academy in 1834. Victoria made several versions of it to be sold for charity, at such functions as 'the Fancy Fair in aid of the Fund for the Relief of Distressed Foreigners' held in Hanover Square.*

Hagar & Ishmael.

a young design

D⁰ directed by M⁰ Westate.

Kábin

1 for Lady L. Jenk

1 for Foreign Dan

1 for d⁰ Westac

1 for D⁰ Buys

Westall has left us one of the most attractive portraits of Victoria ever painted, among the hundreds that were executed in the course of a long and strenuously recorded life. He painted the eleven-year-old Princess with her pencil poised in her hand, holding out her sketching book professionally at arm's length to gauge perspective, her wide-brimmed straw bonnet flung off at her feet. She is sitting in the shade of a tree, by a classical urn, with a running stream beside her. It is an idyllic scene of tranquil rural pleasures, and a fine painting, reflecting the influence of Sir Thomas Lawrence, with whom Westall had lived in the 1790s. But it is without doubt a pretty fantasy. There is no evidence that Princess Victoria was ever allowed out sketching in this carefree manner. Her drawings are strictly schoolroom work, interpretations of books she was reading, such as Walter Scott's *Marmion*, or academic imitations of Westall, or of German artists admired by her mother, such as Moritz Retzsch, whose illustrations of Schiller and Goethe appear regularly in her diary lists of presents received.

Victoria's upbringing was sheltered and closeted, even by those standards that came to be called Victorian. The life of this eldest legitimate descendant of the vast family of George III was infinitely precious; after the death of the Duke of Kent in Victoria's first year the fatherless Princess was closely guarded. Lehzen or the Duchess of Northumberland always sat in on her lessons. Her mother also attended. Victoria recalled in 1872 that she had never had a room of her own, but slept in her mother's room until 1837 when she became Queen. When she went downstairs, her hand was held so that she should not fall; when Leigh Hunt glimpsed her watering flowers in Kensington Garden, he noted that she was followed about by a footman in livery like 'a gigantic fairy'.

When in later years she looked back on her childhood, Queen Victoria always emphasized two aspects: the frugality and the loneliness. In 1872 she wrote: 'We lived in a very simple plain manner . . . Tea was only allowed as a great treat in later years.' To her eldest daughter Vicky, she wrote in 1858: 'I had led a very unhappy life as a child; had no scope

Richard Westall was strongly influenced by the great portraitist Sir Thomas Lawrence, as is shown in this idyllic portrait of the Princess sketching outdoors, with Fanny her favourite dog at her feet.

for my very violent feelings of affection — had no brothers
and sisters to live with — never had a father — from my
unfortunate circumstances was not on a comfortable or at all
intimate or confidential footing with my mother (so different
from you to me) — much as I love her now — and did not
know what a happy domestic life was!'

One of the few people who alleviated this crushing
solitude was her half-sister Feodore, daughter of the Duchess
of Kent by her first marriage to Charles, Prince of Leiningen.
But Feodore was twelve years older than Victoria, and in
1828 she left Kensington Palace for Germany to marry,
leaving Victoria alone with her tutors, Lehzen and Mama. As
Feodore recalled in a letter to the Queen in 1843: 'When I
look back upon those years, which ought to have been the
happiest in my life . . . I cannot help pitying myself. Not to
have enjoyed the pleasures of youth is nothing, but to have
been deprived of all intercourse, and not one cheerful
thought in that dismal existence of ours, was very hard. My

P.V. del
R.P. June 13ᵈ
1837.

Princess of Leiningen,
drawn from nature.

25

only happy time was going or driving out with you and Lehzen; then I could speak and look as I like. I escaped some years of imprisonment, which you, my poor darling sister, had to endure after I was married.'

Because she responded in a way that Mama could not, Feodore received the torrent of Victoria's pent-up emotion. The Duchess of Kent, twice-widowed, a German living for the first time in England, an anxious and overprotective custodian of the future monarch, was an immensely biddable personality, and it was Victoria's great misfortune that her mother chose to be bidden by the self-seeking Sir John Conroy. When Feodore came to stay at Kensington Palace in the summer of 1833, Victoria's fifteenth year, she and her first two children, Eliza and Charles, radiated light and warmth through the gloom and tension. Feodore was a beautiful young woman, with a gentle and serene countenance, large brown eyes and a handsome straight nose, snowy sloping shoulders greatly admired at the time, and a frivolous, beribboned, ornamental taste in clothes and head-dresses. As Victoria recalled later, after Feodore had aged: 'She was very lovely then . . . and had charming manners . . .'

On the day her sister and the two children were leaving, Victoria's skills broke down, but the results convey vividly the extent of her grief. As soon as they had gone she sketched Eliza, in the little shift she had worn as she washed herself that morning, and again, in her travelling dress. In her diary, Victoria raced over fourteen pages — by far the longest entry till her Coronation — as she cried over the pain of parting: 'It is such a VERY VERY GREAT HAPPINESS for me to have my DEAREST most DEARLY BELOVED sister with me in my room . . . How I love her I cannot say . . . It is TOO DREADFUL for me to think that in an hour I shall not see *Dearest* Feodore's *dear kind* sweet face, and the *little beauty* Eliza jumping about, and *good honest* Charles running about the room, any more. . . . I was so dreadfully affected with grief at thinking of parting, that I fell round her [Feodore's] neck and we both cried *bitterly* and pressed each other in our arms *most tenderly*. . . I sobbed and cried most violently the whole morning.'

*Dear little Eliza in her travelling-
dress which she wore the morning
she left us. from nature.*

V. ʃ. Iᵏ P.

Saturday 26ᵗʰ July 1834. The day dearest Feodore went.

When Victoria's half-sister Feodore left after a visit with her two small children in July 1834, the Princess was desolate, and immediately sketched from memory Eliza in her travelling clothes.

Eliza died of tuberculosis, aged twenty, and Victoria, with the coolness of distance and new loves, was able to comment: 'She had rather an unbendable character which made her mother fear she might *not* be happy in the future.' But her earlier effusions had not been merely the expressions of conventional sentimentality; Princess Victoria was clear-sighted in her assessment of character, and never more so when she said that as a child she had no scope for her passionate nature. She was hungry for company, for young company, and her high spirits demanded an outlet. Three years later, when her other half-nephews, Ernest and Edward, the small children of Feodore's brother Charles of Leiningen, came to stay, Victoria again responded with delight at the ordinary demonstrativeness of children: 'Edward was beyond everything funny. He calls me Lisettche, and a number of other odd names. . . . He has no *respect* for me, I fear, at all.' As soon as such visits were over, the stilted tone returned to the diary as she set down the hourly tedium of lessons, interrupted only by mealtimes with the Conroys, rides in the park and ministrations to the many dogs on whom Victoria lavished her starved affections.

The Conroys are ever-present in the daily routine of Kensington Palace; above all, their daughter Victoire, who was a little older than Victoria and was produced, as many unfortunate children are, specifically to be a friend and playmate. She never wins a word of praise or affection from the Princess. She is merely there, and Victoria bleakly states her encroaching ways: 'Victoire stayed from 3 till 6.' 'Victoire dressed here for dinner.' On Victoire's birthday Victoria notes that she went to see her, but says nothing of her gift (if she gave one), though gifts given and received take up large portions of the diary. When they go riding together, Victoria, who rode with the verve she showed in so many other areas, merely comments: 'Victoire rode first on the wrong side Gossamer, then Sylph.'

Right: Victoria craved gaiety: fancy dress provided it, and she and Victoire Conroy, a constant companion, often created costumes out of shawls and borrowed necklaces, and came down to dinner as 'a nun' or 'an old Turkish lawyer' or an 'Italian brigand's wife'.

Dash (our dog.)
From nature. Jan: 11ᵗʰ 1836. *[signature]*

Left: The only thing Sir John Conroy did that Princess Victoria appreciated was to give her mother a King Charles spaniel, Dash. Victoria took him over immediately; when he died she buried him under the epitaph:
Reader
If you would live beloved
And die regretted
Profit by the example of
DASH

A Nun
Sister Victoire

P.V.Rel.
Claremont
16 Jun: 1837.

Portrait of Miss
Victoire Conroy.

P.V. del.
Dec: 1836.
Claremont.

Miss Victoire Conroy
from
nature.

i John Conroy.

The Conroys' likenesses, taken down in the inky silhouettes then fashionable as a parlour game, appear together
in one of Victoria's albums, entitled with unconscious
aptness, 'A Collection of Shades'. The five years recorded in
the diary until the accession, when the whole Conroy tribe
were forbidden to appear at court, show no improvement in
her relations with Victoire, though she continued to pass
some of the enforced hours of her companionship in drawing
portraits of her.

There was one aspect of the 'Kensington System', Sir
John's plan for Victoria's upbringing and his own advancement, that Princess Victoria at first enjoyed. For although
Mama allowed Conroy to persuade her that the heir
presumptive to the throne must not see her royal relations
but be kept aloof from Court, alone at Kensington Palace,
she also agreed with him that Victoria should be seen by her
future subjects. So began in 1832, each autumn, a series of
triumphal progresses through the countryside. King William
IV was infuriated by the honours that Conroy insisted upon:
the royal salutes at Portsmouth — 'the popping must stop',
said the King — the official greetings committees and the
escort of county yeomanry that accompanied the Princess's
carriage. But Victoria, at least to begin with, during the
journey to Wales of 1832, enjoyed getting out and seeing
new people and new sights and making friends, some of
whom remained for life. In this way she made the acquain-
tance of the Pagets, on their estate of Beaudesert. Many
different Pagets were to wait on her as Maids of Honour and
Equerries; at the age of fourteen Victoria enjoyed their
frivolity and sophistication, and Lord Alfred Paget became
one of her favourite dancing partners. Later the clan did not
altogether meet with Albert's approval.

The young Princess proceeded from one great Whig
English country house to another, down roads strewn with
dahlias — for it was October — under arches on which, as she
described, disingenuously trying to disguise her pleasure, her
name was written 'not in ink, but with flowers and pink
bows'. She visited Buxted Park, the seat of Lord Liverpool,

P.V. Bale.
Ramsgate.
23 Oct. 1836.

Lady Catherine Jenkinson.
Drawn from nature.

32

Lady Catherine Jenkinson (left), daughter of Lord Liverpool, often accompanied Victoria on her 'royal progresses' to different parts of England.

Riding was one of the Princess's chief pleasures, and though custom demanded that she ride sidesaddle, she went with greater brio than is suggested by her sketch of a riding party (below right) in decorous Tunbridge Wells.

and met his daughters the Ladies Louisa and Selina Jenkinson, who played the harp and the piano after dinner and gave excerpts from operas. Louisa was later a train-bearer at her Coronation, and Lord Liverpool was the only Tory — with the august exception of the Duke of Wellington — who was invited to her wedding, for through the friendship formed during these early years he understood the Princess's abilities and supported her against Conroy. At Chatsworth she watched a charade, her first encounter with a game that met all her love of gaiety and dressing up and later became a staple entertainment of her family gatherings. The word 'Kenilworth', from Scott's novel, was mimed in four costume tableaux, and the characters recorded in her sketchbook. On a visit to Hardwicke Hall nearby, she saw the window through which Mary Queen of Scots was spied upon, and noted it was 'very singular'.

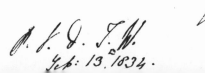

A riding party.

o. v. d. J. W.
Feb: 13. 1834.

P. V. J. Oct: 30^t 1832.

Pitchford.

Last scene of

34

charade el Chatworth

Deceased Queens were not the only objects of the Princess's curious scrutiny. She complained to Uncle Leopold when he sent her an extract about the government of Queen Anne: '[I] must beg you, as you have sent me to show what a Queen *ought not* to be, that you will send me what a Queen *ought to be.*' She had met Donna Maria da Gloria, Queen of Portugal, at a children's party given by King George IV, but Victoria was only eight years old at the time. When she met her again, in Portsmouth during a yachting trip, Victoria was fourteen, and she noted Donna Maria and her stepmother the ex-Empress of Brazil, then only twenty-one, with some care, and made drawings on her sketch pad. 'Donna Maria', she wrote, 'is only a month older than I am

Previous page: Staying at Chatsworth House in Derbyshire in the autumn of 1832, Victoria saw her first game of charades played by the large house party. She did not take part, but the occasion made a vivid impression on her and tableaux vivants *remained a favourite pastime all her life.*

Victoria observed with close interest two young queens whom she met when she was fourteen: Amelia, the ex-Empress of Brazil (left), and her 'very stout' stepdaughter Donna Maria da Gloria of Portugal (below right).

and is very kind to me . . . she is grown very tall but also very stout . . . She has a beautiful complexion, and is very sweet and friendly. She wore her hair in two large curls in front and a thick fine plait turned up behind. The Empress . . . has beautiful blue eyes, and has a fine tall figure . . . She was simply dressed in a grey watered moiré trimmed with blonde.' Artlessly, and with perfect good nature, the girl who knew she would one day be Queen of England was taking stock of the first two young queens she had ever met. Four years later, and more discerning, Victoria disliked comment on the 'likeness' between herself and Donna Maria, for Maria's education was 'one of the worst that could be.'

P. Voil.
Vov: 1836. Ramsgate.

Boulogne fishermen
from recollection.

The scarring of early industrial England was not lost on the Princess as her carriage bowled along towards the great ancestral houses, but her instinct was to dismiss such ugliness. Though she drew her fellow passengers, and the horses' dancing heads from the carriage, she did not record the figures of misery which she must have seen on her travels. But in the course of a stay at St Leonards, during which the boredom of the repetitious days hangs pall-like over the diary, Victoria's fount of strong feelings was again tapped. There had been a shipwreck off the coast and six men had drowned. Victoria, like a newspaper reader today, was hungry for more details of adversity. 'The wind blows a hurricane, the sea is mountains high and deluges of rain', she wrote. 'Another body of one of the poor men was found quite close here this morning, and they carried it past the windows.' When by chance, out walking with Lehzen, the Princess saw one of the widows, she was fascinated: 'Mrs Covely . . . stood on the steps. She had a cheerful countenance with rosy cheeks and fine teeth. She was in deep mourning and had a widow-cap on.'

39

The disconsolate

1st L. pt d.
2d Jan 1835.

Mrs Covely went straight into the sketchbook; but so did an imaginary figure, inscribed 'The Disconsolate'. Ignoring the 'blooming and cheerful appearance' of Mrs Covely as unfitting, Victoria summoned up that persistent morbidity that was to become one of her most difficult and dominating traits of character. Yet Mrs Covely is one of the very few people Victoria drew outside her own narrow circle. She was not in the least haughty, and at times showed strong powers of empathy, but this natural responsiveness seems to have been staunched in later life.

Just before she became Queen, she made friends with a family of gipsies encamped on the road near Claremont House, the English home of her uncle Leopold. She was

Sarah Cooper
Gipsy woman near
Claremont.
from recollection

P.V. del.
Claremont
Dec: 1836.

41

P. V. del.
Dec: 12th 1836.
Claremont.

Gipsey women near Claremont.
from recollection.
(The same women as on the other side.)

P.V. del:
Claremont.
Acc: 1836.

Gipsy woman & children
near Claremont.
from recollection.

The woman called Sarah Cooper & the
children (her nephew & nieces) called: Dinah,
Job, Britannia, Emmeline, Helen &c.

deeply stirred by them, and became their impassioned defender. When a baby was born to one of the young women, Victoria made certain that food and blankets were provided. Though the child had no father, she wanted to call him Leopold after her uncle, but dared not suggest it, not because she thought it improper for a bastard — she never gives an inkling of such prejudice — but because the gipsies did not ask her to be sponsor. 'It is *atrocious*', she wrote in high indignation in 1837, 'how often these poor creatures have been falsely accused, cruelly wronged, and greatly ill-treated.'

The gipsies distracted her from life at home. Kensington Palace was silent, gloomy and tense, and she passed most of her 'very unhappy life as a child' shut up inside it. But even the Conroys did not prevent her — though they almost always came with her — from discovering the intoxicating interest, the abiding elation of 'the Play'.

Mme Taglioni, as la Sylphide & others. Albert as James,
as they
appeared in the ballet of la Sylphide
at the King's Theatre this season.

P.V.1.
K.P.
June 20
1832.

TWO

Souvenirs
de l'Opéra

Princess Victoria was stagestruck. She is perhaps the first little girl on record, and certainly the most august, to have languished for the heroines of the boards with the intense identification described in such classics as *Ballet Shoes*. For London in the late 1820s and 1830s saw the flowering of romantic ballet; to London came the most celebrated interpreters of Italian opera, then in its salad days with Bellini, Rossini, Donizetti; here too was carried on the lively tradition of melodrama, performed with full-blooded gusto by the spirited heirs of Kean and Kemble. Victoria was there, sometimes as often as three times a week, sitting in her box after dinner, surrounded by her faithful retinue of Mama, Lehzen and the Conroys. Day after day in her diary she copies out playbills, dashes off enthusiastic summaries of plots and highlights, despatches an ugly actress with a single blow, or enthuses fulsomely about her favourites. The young critic's ready-reckoner of praise was simple: 'I was very much amused', closes her account of an evening's pleasure; or 'I was *very very much amused*', or 'I was VERY VERY MUCH AMUSED' (two underlinings), or 'I WAS VERY VERY MUCH AMUSED INDEED' (three underlinings).

Marie Taglioni, 'goddess of the dance', was the creator and personification of romantic ballet.

47

By the time she was fourteen, Victoria was in thrall to ballet. Over half her collection of dolls consists of dancers in different roles, and these are, contrary to common belief, almost the only real characters she brought to life in this way. The other dolls, given grandiose names and stories — the thrice-married Harriet Arnold, Duchess of Parma, and the twin-bearing Countess of Rothesay — are imaginary. But the ballerinas whom she saw inhabited the ethereal sphere fit for dolls, and she and Lehzen together made a troupe from tiny five-inch Dutch figurines, dressed them in miniature

Miss Woolford, one of the first circus dancers, was married to Andrew Ducrow, the eccentric and tempestuous creator of the modern circus spectacular.

My del — 1845. *Mazourka. 1ᵐᵉ*

In Eoline, ou La Dryade, *a ballet Victoria saw at Her Majesty's in 1845, Eoline is bewitched by her wicked lover the gnome Rubezahl, and 'like the bird fascinated by a serpent . . . yields'. Together they dance 'a fantastic mazourka', the Mazourka d'Extase.*

replicas of the costumes they had worn on stage, and arranged them in pairs according to their favourite ballet stories. Tiny rosettes of ribbon, edgings of gold braid, pinafores of veiling, cross-laced corsages, silk slippers a quarter of an inch long, head-dresses with beads and plumes, minute reticules attached to wrists, bandeaux set with a gem — all were worked by Lehzen with the Princess's assistance, or sometimes by Victoria herself, supervised by the governess. They formed a strikingly charming catalogue of the contemporary ballet repertory, and in particular of Victoria's idol, the greatest ballerina of her day and the creator of the romantic sublime in nineteenth-century dance, Marie Taglioni.

49

Pt. 2. To P.
July 13th 1834.
as she appeared in the   Mlle Taglioni
                        ballet of Le Pouvoir de la danse ou la Nouvelle
                                                                        Therbichon

'Lehzen finished for me . . . at about 6, a lovely doll, representing La Sylphide, which I saw in town', writes the Princess in her Journal. The ballet *La Sylphide*, the prototype of the 'ballet blanc', was created for Taglioni by her father Filippo, the most inventive and dedicated choreographer of his day. For the role, Eugène Lami designed the costume that has become synonymous with romantic ballet: the multi-layered white skirt of tulle, caught into a satin bodice and cut off at the knee so that the dancers' legs are seen.

Marie Taglioni was half Italian, half Swedish. She was trained by her father, and became the pioneer of dancing on points. 'She danced quite beautifully, quite as if she flew in the air, so gracefully and lightly', wrote Victoria after seeing her in *La Sylphide*. 'When she bounds and skips along the stage, it is quite beautiful. Quite like a fawn. And she has grace in every action. The motion of her arms and beautiful hands are so graceful, and she has such a sweet expression in her face . . .' Later, making a literary effort, the Princess commented: 'It seemed as if some sylph had taken her form and lighted upon earth.'

Victoria was not alone in her delight: Taglioni's new technique inspired her audience to an extent rarely achieved by avant-garde revolutions in the arts. Thackeray wrote to his mother from Paris: 'They have a superb dancing damsel yclept Taglioni who hath the most superb pair of pins, & maketh the most superb use of them that ever I saw dancer do before. Then there is Paul [Taglioni, Marie's brother and frequent partner] who will leap you quite off the per- pendicular & on the horizontal & recover his feet with the greatest dexterity.' Victor Hugo dedicated a book '*A vos pieds, à vos ailes*'. Berlioz, seeing Taglioni at the height of her international fame in 1843, was no less transported by 'this gentle and melancholy joy, this chaste passion, this swallow's flight over the surface of a lake'. The first company to run coaches between London and Windsor in two hours painted Marie Taglioni on the doors of their vehicles; Victoria herself named a new fast horse after the dancer. When the Princess's dolls had been put away as childish things, she took to fancy dress for dinner: 'I dressed myself up as La Naiade, as Taglioni was dressed, with corals in my hair'.

Victoria's love of Taglioni was not only composed of admiration for her agility and her gentle 'all-ways smiling' countenance. Taglioni was ethereal and vulnerable, modest, even austere. The Parisian chant, '*Est-ce femme, ou est-ce l'air?*' accurately reflects Taglioni's almost spiritual appeal, her fulfilment of the aesthetic ideal of disembodied existence. Victoria was not incapable of earthier tastes: she admired, for example, Taglioni's principal rival, Fanny Essler — famed for the vigorous sensuality of her interpretations — in her most passionate role of all, the Cachucha, with castanets. But usually she found Essler coarse. Taglioni's combination of excellence and naivety tallied exactly with Victoria's con- ception of womanliness to which, contrary to the wilfulness and impetuosity of her nature, she would like to have conformed.

A fascinating aspect of the romantic ballet is that it embodied a fragile, often doomed, ideal of the feminine while choosing as themes rousing stories of struggle. Taglioni

Marie Taglioni was idolized but not idealized by Victoria. Her blend of sweetness, austerity, naivety and skill had the quality of genius. 'She ha grace in every action', wrote her worshipper. 'The motion of her arms and beautiful hands is so graceful, and she has such a mild sweet expression i her face.'

Mlle Taglioni as La Sylphide.   P.V.I. 1833

P.V. f. 14 P.
March 20th
1832
Mlle Duvernay as she appeared as [illegible]
Pas de schalls, in the ballet [illegible] of the maid
of Cashmere.

created *The Revolt of the Harem*, which set a minor fashion for ballets portraying female emancipation in exotic settings — in this case, the Alhambra. Victoria saw another dancer, Mrs Honey, in *The Revolt of the Naiades* and was much taken with the Amazon scenes: 'The scenery is excessively pretty and the scenes of the coral retreat, of the Naiades bathing, the Stalactistic Hall with the Fête of the Water Queen, and the Revolt and Jeu de guerre are quite beautiful', she wrote. This evening at the Adelphi rated three underscorings.

But the ballet that concentrated all aspects of the formula dear to Victoria was *Le Dieu et la Bayadère, or The Maid of Cashmere*, to music by Auber. Victoria sketched both Taglioni and Pauline Duvernay, whom she also much admired, in the principal role. Her favourite scene came at

Victoria painted Pauline Duvernay after seeing her do the shawl dance from Le Dieu et la Bayadère *to music by Auber.*

54

the end, when the 'unknown' man in the palanquin reveals himself to be the 'god', rescues the maiden, and 'takes her up to heaven'. Far away settings, barbarian costumes, exquisite and faint-hearted heroines, toweringly heroic males materializing at the last minute, put the young girl soon to be Queen into a state of blissful surrender.

In the nineteenth century it was the fashion to vary the evening's entertainment in the theatre. In one night — the benefit or gala of an artiste, for example — she might see part of an opera, some solo arias, a *tour de force* from one ballet and a scene from another, performed by the foremost interpreters, themselves versatile. After dinner Victoria and her party would leave Kensington Palace to take their seats in their usual box after the curtain had gone up. As a rule they rose before the end, though the Princess was often enjoying herself so much that she left with reluctance.

Heberlé, a pioneer interpreter of romantic roles, had 'immense force and power', wrote Victoria, who saw her only once; she 'was like a young deer in her actions, but her style was quite different to Taglioni's.'

55

P.V. del. Feb.
April 1837.

Mr. Charles Mathews's
as Dapperwit in The Rape
of the Lock.

*Charles Mathews (left),
here in the role of
Dapperwit in John
Oxenford's adaptation of
The Rape of the Lock,
was in Victoria's opinion
'the most delightful and
amusing actor possible'.
With his wife Eliza
Vestris, he evolved a new
informal and naturalistic
style of acting, in such
comedies as Riquet with
the Tuft (right), written
for them by Charles
Dance and James Planché.*

One inspired impresario who struggled gamely for many
years in different theatres against appalling financial odds was
Eliza Vestris. At the Olympic, Madame Vestris produced
plays, cast them, acted and sang herself, and invited dancers
and singers to provide divertissements between the acts.
Victoria's loyalty to her and to her husband, the actor Charles
Mathews, lasted until Vestris's death in 1856; she went often
to see them perform, and invited them to Windsor for
private theatricals. Her taste in such matters was sound. Even
Lord Melbourne, always cutting and usually bored by the
theatre, commented about Vestris: 'It's very rare to see a
good actress. It's very rare to see a good anything, that's the
fact.'

P.S. del. N.V.

April 16th 1837. (from recollection) Mme Vestris - as Belinda. &c —

Victoria admired (and drew) the best-looking and the most accomplished performers: Ellen Tree, who '*acted very well indeed*' in *The Red Mask, or the Council of Three*, a historical melodrama by James Robinson Planché; Fanny Kemble — not as Juliet, the role in which she made her spectacular début, but as Lady Macbeth in which she was also a great success; John Cooper, who 'looked EXTREMELY WELL' in Addison's forgotten drama about Henri IV, *The King's Seal;* and other famous names, Charles Mathews and Charles Macready. But Victoria's judgement was not always reliable. After she saw the famous production of Shakespeare's *King John* for which Planché designed costumes that for the first time aimed at historical verisimilitude, *King John* always ranked in her estimation above *King Lear* or *Hamlet*.

One of the very few Shakespearean scenes she drew is the famous final submission of Katherina in *The Taming of the Shrew*. The dramatic contest for mastery between a strong woman and a strong man appealed to her, as did the play's lesson, that males prevail. In later life Victoria liked to reiterate that the proper order of nature had been reversed by her queenship and precedence over Albert.

Catherine Petruchio

Mr. Bennett, as Grindoff, the Miller, & Miss Taylor
born off by Grindoff in the "Miller
his Men." in the 2 act. ✗ (Claudine

Victoria's sketchpad recalls high moments of melodrama: she was inspired for instance by the death-defying selflessness of the noble savage Rolla, hero of *Pizarro*, Sheridan's rodomontade against the Spaniards. One of the best parts, she thought, was 'when he comes on all bleeding and places the rescued child in Cora's arms and falls down dead.' The blowing-up of the powder magazine at the end of *The Miller and His Men*, a family favourite by Isaac Pocock with music by Henry Bishop, earned several underlinings and a sequence of excited drawings. The dialogue of the last scene is characteristic:

Grindoff, robber-king and villain of Isaac Pocock's melodrama The Miller and His Men, *abducts the senseless heroine into his mountain lair (above). But Lothair, hero and true lover, anticipates his every*

60

move and saves Claudine (above right); as they make their escape Grindoff's hideaway is blown up, with all his banditti followers trapped inside.

Wolf:	(*With a shout of great exultation*) Ha! Ha! You strive in vain!
Karl:	Cowardly rascal! You will be caught at last. (*Shaking his sword at Wolf*)
Wolf:	By whom?
Karl:	Your only friend, Beelzebub . . .
Wolf:	Foolhardy slave, I have sworn never to descend from the spot alive, unless with liberty.

The spot, his robber's lair, explodes, dynamited by Karl and his righteous supporters.

P.V. del.
Dec: 26.ʰ
1836.ᵗʰ
Claremont
1836.

Mˡˡᵉ Duvernay as
Florinda,
in "the Devil on two sticks."
1ˢᵗ Act.
from recollection.

Henry Crabb Robinson, who kept an ardent amateur's diary of theatregoing from 1811 to 1866, commented as a specialist in 'horrid' spectacles: 'The melodrama of *The Miller and His Men* interested me as all Banditti occurrences do. The scenes however — and in such pieces these are the most material parts of the exhibition — are not so horrid as I have seen before. And the plot is not so well contrived. In such pieces a gross and palpable probability is a great requisite. And here one does not see . . . what end is answered to blow up the magazine at last.' When Victoria took Prince Albert, whose stomach was much more refined, to a revival, she records in all ingenuousness that he said he was interested but kept his praise for the music.

Victoria's interest in the theatre did not wane as she grew older, but it never reached the intensity of her girlhood passion for the ballet. Ballet and opera were mixed in the long programmes offered by Drury Lane, the King's Theatre, and later Covent Garden, and from the age of about fifteen onwards the Princess's affections gradually shifted from Taglioni towards the greatest singer of the day, Giulia Grisi. Taglioni was sadly neglected. Indeed Queen Victoria does not seem to have been aware that her childhood idol was scraping a living in the 1870s giving lessons in 'social dances and deportment for the aristocracy', or that she died in poverty in 1884. In 1837, Victoria, chafing at a long exile from London during the season, had written to Uncle Leopold: 'we shall have been *six months* in the country next Thursday . . . and I am sure you will stand by me for my having my seasons fully, as you may understand that my *Operatic* and *Terpsichorean* feelings are pretty strong . . .' But she was certain that she preferred 'the Opera by far to the ballet. Grisi far surpasses Taglioni in my estimation.'

Grisi's ascent to the position of *prima donna assoluta* marks a moment in the history of opera as revolutionary as Taglioni's use of the first padded ballet shoe in the history of ballet. In both cases Victoria was there, enthusiastic, spontaneous and committed. She spent £600 in one year — 1839 — on her boxes. Three quarto albums in the Royal Library at Windsor

63

Signor Rubini, Signora Grisi & M. Ivanoff,
Neocles, Pamira & Cleomene.
(L'Assiedo di Corinto)
O.K.d. K.P.
June 27th 1834.

Signora Grisi   & M. Ivanoff
Pamira   as   Cleomene.
(in L'Assiedo di Corinto.)
J.K.f. K.P.
June 27th

record the Princess's impressions. Volume I is inscribed in a careful copperplate hand over pencilled rules:

Souvenirs de l'Opéra
Sketches from Recollection
MLLE. Giulietta Grisi &c.
by P.V.
1835
1836

Inside, Victoria pasted drawings of figures from the productions she saw, from operas still in repertory today — Bellini's *Norma* and *I Puritani*, Donizetti's *L'Elisir d'Amore*, Rossini's *Cenerentola* and *La Gazza Ladra* — but also from entirely forgotten works, such as Rossini's *Otello* which was eclipsed by Verdi's later version; the Italian-born composer Michael Costa's *Malek Adel*, with a crusader theme; and the Irishman Michael Balfe's *Maid of Artois*, written specially for the legendary singer La Malibran. Victoria's drawings are

The modern tradition of faithful, historical costuming in opera was begun in Victoria's time. In 1834 she saw the première of Rossini's L'Assiedo di Corinto *and noted carefully (above) Grisi's plaits, Ivanoff's scimitar and turban, Rubini's Greek bolero and skirt, and (right) the splendid eastern exoticism of the famous bass Tamburini in the role of Mahomet, Emperor of the Turks.*

64

repetitive, for as she always sat in the same box, her vantage point for sketch after sketch was identical. Clumsy as they are, they constitute a fascinating souvenir of the performers, their costumes and gestures. It is a sad loss to theatre history that settings interested her so little, for she rarely drew scenery. It was the human voice as an instrument for expressing emotion that bound her to opera.

Signor Tamburini & Mdme G. Grisi
as
Mahomet & Pamira
in l'Assedio di Corinto. P.V.d.S.P.
June 22d 1834.

Victoria's first interest in opera coincided with the emergence of the soprano as the dominant solo performer. Grisi's glory was made possible by the death in 1836 of the then unsurpassed Malibran, otherwise Maria Felicitá García; she died suddenly in Manchester at the age of twenty-eight. Malibran was a natural contralto, but her father, the Spanish tenor Manuel García, had trained her to add a soprano's super-register, giving her a voice of extraordinary range. Malibran intoxicated her audiences: her low notes, held very very long, were thrilling; her impassioned renderings — she tore her glove to shreds as Mary Queen of Scots in Donizetti's *Maria Stuarda* — shocked and enthralled those who heard her. The cruel struggle between the castrato singer, who had hitherto dominated opera — and topped the bill — and the emergent soprano is well caught by an anecdote of Malibran's début in London at the age of sixteen. The castrato Velluti was so scared that she would outshine him on stage that he would only sing plain notes in rehearsal. But Malibran, hearing his embellishments for the first time during the performance, copied them effortlessly, adding several florid decorations of her own. '*Briccona*' (rascal), hissed the poor castrato in the girl's ear.

That was in 1824. A decade later, at Princess Victoria's sixteenth birthday concert, a present from her mother and surely one of the most dazzling collections of musical talent ever made for a private recital, there was no thought of inviting a castrato. The fashion for their particular timbre and tone was over. Instead Malibran, Grisi and all the other great interpreters — Luigi Lablache the bass, Rubini, Tamburini and Ivanoff — performed for Victoria. Malibran arrived late, 'dressed in white satin with a scarlet hat and feathers'. Victoria noted: 'Her low notes are *beautiful*, but her high notes are thick and not clear. I like *Grisi by far better* than her.' Malibran's sudden death stunned her hundreds of *aficionados*, and intense poetic tributes such as Alfred de Musset's 'Stances à la Malibran' commemorated her gift. Even Queen Victoria conceded that 'in point of cleverness and genius there is not a doubt that Malibran far surpassed Grisi . . . '

Above: The voice of La Malibran was the most famous in Europe at the time of her premature death in 1836, the year Victoria drew this portrait.

Right: Victoria thought that Norma in Bellini's famous opera was her adored Giulia Grisi's best role.

66

Mme Grisi - as - Norma & Mlle Assandri - as Adalgisa.
in Norma. — Finale to 1st Act:

P.V. del.
1836.-

But Grisi was her favourite, not least because of her beauty. Victoria was delighted when she saw the singer out riding in the Park: 'She is pale off the stage, but has not at all a delicate appearance. On the contrary she has a very slight pinkish hue over her face. She looks very pretty and mild.' Three days later, at the première of Donizetti's *Marino Faliero* (based on Byron's play), Victoria was gripped by Grisi's intensity: 'Elena then stares wildly about her, her hand raised to her head, and giving a frantic scream falls prostrate and lifeless to the ground . . . I know no singer I like as well as Grisi. She is perfection (to my feeling). She is *very pretty* and is

Mme Grisi as Elena in Marino Faliero.
Act 3ᵈ. Scene 1ˢᵗ. Elena. "Dio clemenza."

The poet Théophile Gautier said that under Grisi's spell opera was transformed into a tragedy and a poem. Victoria could never see or hear her enough, and remained alive to every nuance of the singer's famous powers of intensely emotional expression.

Above: Albertazzi, an English soprano whom Victoria admired for 'her voice of great compass', seen here as the Crusader in Malek Adel *by Michael Costa.*

Above right: Victoria was upset when Grisi, in the role of Elena in Donizetti's Marino Faliero, *'did not look quite so pretty as usual, as she had combed her hair too low into her face . . . '*

an *exquisite* singer and *charming* actress!' She was enraptured by Grisi's generosity in applauding warmly a rival, Albertazzi — now forgotten — in Rossini's *Cinderella*. 'She is a good-natured creature, Grisi', wrote her adorer. A special bow Grisi made to her box gave her the greatest pleasure, and the singer's appearance in person at her birthday treat, 'that delicious concert', inspired a litany of adulation. 'Such a lovely mild expression . . . such beautiful dark eyes with fine long eyelashes . . . Her beautiful dark hair . . . She is very quiet, ladylike and unaffected in her manners.' Victoria dressed herself for a ball with 'a wreath of white roses like Grisi has in the Puritani' — her favourite opera, usually referred to as '*dear* Puritani'.

The singers Grisi, Lablache, Rubini and Tamburini became known as 'the Puritani Quartet' after their unrivalled collaboration in Bellini's emotive Romeo and Juliet story set in Roundhead England. The member of the Quartet whom Victoria came to know best was Luigi Lablache, the monumental basso. Lablache had a genius for *opera buffa*

*Left: Luigi Lablache,
creator of the title role of
the Doge in* Marino
Faliero.

At this stage in her
artistic development,
Victoria was using a
limited watercolour box.
The striking purple of
Lablache's cloak is an
early example of her
blending different colours.

*Below: Again and again,
the fatherless Victoria
drew the scene from
Rossini's* Otello *in which
Desdemona finds that
everyone, even her father,
has lost faith in her.*

roles, to which his great size but nimbleness suited him, as well as for *opera seria*, in which, as the Druid in *Norma* or the leading Roundhead in *I Puritani*, he dominated majestically. Although Lablache delighted the Princess, he did not make her heart flutter as Grisi did. Yet she drew him more often than any other figure. One particular scene from Rossini's *Otello* recurs many times: Lablache towering over the tiny figure of Grisi as Desdemona while she pleads for understanding from her father Elmiro. '*Se il padre m'abbandona, da chi sperar pietà?*' ('If ever my father abandons me, from whom else can I hope for pity?') was a line carved deep in Victoria's memory, it seems. Once again her imagination was captured by a scene of female vulnerability, intensified here by Desdemona's psychological orphanhood. Victoria, who chose to write to Uncle Leopold in Italian that he was not just 'il mio secondo padre', but '*solo* padre', seems to have felt for the plight of the fatherless children around whom the plots of so many romantic operas are built. Amina, Grisi's role in Bellini's *Sonnambula* — one of Victoria's favourite operas — is a foster-child; Norma's lover Pollione, by whom she has two children, leaves them orphans not through his death, but his infidelity.

It would be misleading to give a neurotic edge to Victoria's love of romantic opera. She revelled in its humour too, liking particularly Lablache's Don Magnifico in *Cinderella*, and his comic improvisations in the one-act *opera buffa* by Gnecco, *La Prova di una Opera Seria*. Almost incoherent with pleasure, Victoria described the scenes: 'Signor Lablache was *beyond* every thing! He looked so funny, in his huge powdered wig and bad brown silk coat and sword. And acted — Oh! *inimitably*! He personated the distracted composer when Corilla [Grisi] sings out of tune *exquisitely* . . . When he . . . walks with bent legs . . . and imitates her voice; she then does the same to him, and they both dance. Grisi valsed about the stage by herself in a *very funny manner* . . . Lablache kept us continually laughing . . .'

When Victoria learned that the Vernon family, whom she met on her journeys in the north of England, had been

receiving lessons from Tamburini, her resolve to be taught properly herself must have stiffened. In 1836 Lablache himself came to Kensington Palace, and for twenty years continued to coach the high small voice of the Queen with his huge, deep, rolling bass. Lablache was endlessly good natured. Victoria recorded her appreciation: 'He is so good-humoured, and though tired, or bored (as I should think he must often be, by teaching a person like me, all the lovely songs &c, which he hears Grisi, Rubini &c. sing) he is always even-tempered, merry and most obliging . . . I liked my lesson extremely.' He had parts transposed to suit Victoria's voice, and patiently took her and Mama through the great arias. Victoria discussed music earnestly with him; she felt unable to agree about Mozart's supreme superiority. 'I am a terribly modern person', she wrote, 'and I must say I prefer Bellini, Rossini, Donizetti, etc, to anything else; but Lablache, who *understands* music *thoroughly*, said, "C'est le Papa de tous".' To her astonishment, Victoria discovered that her

P. V. f. Oct: 1832.

Rosina

Lablache.
from recollection.

P.V. del:—
Kensington
Palace Aug: 1836.

hero — with whom she spoke French — was half Irish. His father was French and he was born in Naples, where several of his enormous family were being brought up.

She also discovered, and her report has a slightly puzzled air, that Lablache did not share her own high opinion of Grisi, but criticized the singer's way of swallowing before a roulade — 'a habit she has contracted from fear of failing . . . I do not think he quite *likes* her'. Indeed, when the mercurial impresario Alfred Bunn removed all the greatest singers from the King's Theatre to his new establishment at Covent Garden in 1847, Lablache refused to follow Grisi, Mario and the others. But even Lablache's reservations about Grisi could not dim her attraction for Victoria. Grisi remained the touchstone by which she judged all the great singers of the century, although slightly grudgingly she did admit later that Jenny Lind eclipsed her favourite.

Grisi never became the Queen's friend; perhaps her teenage idolatry made such a relationship impossible. Lablache, on the other hand, was the first of many to gain Victoria's impetuous affections, and to earn that high mark of her attachment: that she was really, though she knew she must not be, 'quite cross' when he could not come. Lord Melbourne and Prince Albert were Lablache's successors in this accolade of the young Queen's impatience.

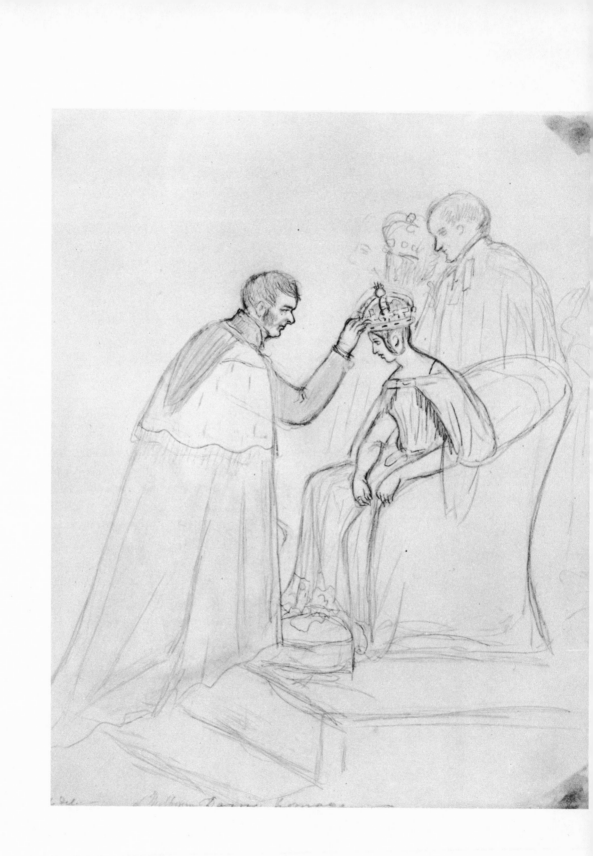

THREE

'His Dear, Dear Face'

Lord Melbourne, who was Prime Minister when Victoria became Queen in 1837, did not like birdsong and could not distinguish a woodlark from a nightingale. He preferred the singing of blackbirds anyway; best of all, he liked the cawing of rooks and could watch them for hours as they circled at sunset. Victoria was surprised by this; she disliked their grating and insistent calling. 'The rooks are my delight', declared Lord Melbourne. Albert on the other hand loved the song of nightingales. Queen Victoria remembered later how he would listen for them 'in the happy peaceful walks he used to take with the Queen in the woods', and whistle to them 'in their own peculiar long note', so that they would reply in kind. On summer evenings he led her out on to the balcony at Osborne to hear them.

Rooks and nightingales: both played their part in Victoria's sensibility. She was down-to-earth, impatient of nonsense, fascinated by unembellished fact, quick to laugh 'till her gums showed', and inclined to gobble her food. But she also had a strong romantic strain, which made her less robust, less humorous, more volatile. Melbourne was a survivor of the last century's sanguine, savoury nonchalance; his laconic wit was the epitome of aristocratic Whiggishness. Albert, whom she was to marry less than three years after she became Queen, was a blueprint of nineteenth-century German romanticism, emotional, serious, high-minded, diligent and often tormented.

At her Coronation Victoria found the homage of all the peers 'a pretty ceremony': 'they first of all touch the Crown, and then kiss my hand.'

77

As a young woman, Victoria was soft wax; the mixture was by nature very strong, but at the time of her accession she was ready, almost longing, to take the impress of any powerful stamp. She liked male company, and she had a gift for intimacy: she responded warmly, loved to listen, learned quickly and was flatteringly impressionable. Lord Melbourne and Prince Albert were strongly contrasted, but each, in his singular way, was a remarkable mentor.

The entry in her Journal for 20 June 1837, the day Victoria became Queen, uses the word 'alone' with defiant stress. She was *alone*, not even Mama was present, during the famous dawn encounter when the Archbishop of Canterbury and Lord Conyngham told the eighteen-year-old girl that King William IV was dead 'and consequently that I am *Queen*'.

Three hours later, Lord Melbourne came. 'I saw [him] in my room and of *course* quite *alone* as I shall *always* do all my Ministers. He kissed my hand ...' Victoria liked him immediately, and from then on Melbourne fills the pages of her Journal — Melbourne talking, joking, gossiping, instructing, clarifying, helping, reassuring, encouraging, enlivening; a brilliant, droll, individual mind forming that of a simple, ingenuous young woman forty years his junior. Victoria reported his conversation with the fidelity of Boswell, catching his inimitable caustic phrasing with a genuine diarist's gift of recall. The figure of Lord Melbourne crowds out all others at this time. The past is purged: Mama's bed is moved out of the Queen her daughter's room.

In 1841, Melbourne confided to Albert that when he first met the Queen he had been taken aback at how ill-equipped and immature she was and how urgently she needed guidance on all subjects. But the charm of his nature prevented any such opinion being communicated to Victoria. For the first time, she met a man steeped in the savoir-faire and culture of that most worldly-wise of societies, the London of Byron and the Prince Regent, and this man gave her his whole attention. Slowly and casually, without larding the compliments, he increased her confidence. He trusted her with stories about her rakish family, the royal uncles from

Lord Melbourne, Queen Victoria's first Prime Minister, made the early months of her reign 'the pleasantest summer I ever passed in my life'. 'The more I see of him and the more I know of him,' she wrote, 'the more I like and appreciate his fine and honest character'.

whom her mother had so jealously screened her. When she worried about her height, he reassured her: 'I lamented my being so short, which Lord M. smiled at and thought no misfortune.' He praised her 'fine character' when she told him she had never lied, though she was 'a passionate and naughty child'. He told her dry and wonderfully funny anecdotes about everyone from Napoleon to Robert Walpole to Queen Anne. Melbourne was the only person with whom she felt '*safe*': '*He alone* inspires me with that feeling of great confidence and I may say security . . . '

The young Queen absorbed Lord Melbourne's views on matters trivial and grave with equal interest: through her diary we know that he told her 'trees never grew so well in Ireland and were all a little bent from the wind blowing across the Atlantic', but we know too that this very experienced, subtle, discerning man took immense pains to lead Victoria to understand government, and that he was the only person to do so at the time. He undertook her first political education, a duty that he discharged in the main with wisdom, a light touch, inimitable tact and profound responsibility.

They saw each other every day, and both were the happier for it. In each case, the friendship was a sudden brightness: Lord Melbourne's rich prospects of happiness had been ruined by his marriage to the erratic Lady Caroline Lamb, who died in 1828, a year before their only son. Melbourne had no child, Victoria no father. Charles Greville, the diarist, thought their love unconsciously sexual, but realised the degree of frustrated family feeling on both sides. 'I have no doubt he is passionately fond of her as he might be of his daughter if he had one; and the more because he is a man with a capacity for loving without having anything in the world to love'. But ambiguous relations, neither blood nor contract, are always socially disturbing. The crowd booed Victoria at Ascot. 'Mrs Melbourne', they called.

When in 1839 Victoria faced the loss of Melbourne as her Prime Minister, to be replaced by Sir Robert Peel, she panicked. Then took place what has come to be known as the

Lady Flora Hastings, whose silhouette Victoria pasted into an album, was one of her mother's ladies-in-waiting. But she was also a friend of the Conroy family, and the Princess allowed her personal dislike of Lady Flora to colour her judgement. She suspected publicly the young woman of pregnancy (she was unmarried) and when Lady Flora died in 1839 of an internal tumour, the scandal cost Victoria her early popularity.

Bedchamber Plot. Peel wished for the dismissal of the Whig ladies who were Melbourne's friends and surrounded Victoria; the Queen was affronted by this interference with her personal entourage. Melbourne rallied the Cabinet to support her, and remained in power.

Whether Melbourne manipulated the Queen to his own advantage or not, her terror of losing him was certainly genuine. It is written into every syllable of her letter to him at the height of the crisis, in which she plays havoc with syntax and pronouns: 'He [Peel] said he couldn't expect me to have the confidence in him I had in you (and which he never can have) . . . The Queen don't like his manner after — oh! how different, how dreadfully different, to that frank, open, natural and most kind, warm manner of Lord Melbourne . . . The Queen was very much collected, and betrayed no agitation during these two trying audiences. But afterwards again *all* gave way . . . what is worst of all is the being deprived of seeing Lord Melbourne as she used to.' She did not lose him, this time.

For most of the first three years of her reign, Victoria's watercolour box and pencils lay idle. But when she did take up her pencil, very often her subject was Lord Melbourne. His handsome, rumpled face appears again and again, on loose sheets, on blotting paper, in the margin of unfinished letters, sometimes in the scarlet and blue Windsor uniform in which Victoria specially admired him, sometimes playing with one of her dogs.

When she set down, in a thin album bound in marbled paper, a few memorial sketches of her Coronation, Melbourne was the protagonist of her imagination. The execution of other figures, and the faces of other participants (including her own) is often clumsy and lazy, but over Melbourne's features she lingered painstakingly. She wrote in her diary that she was deeply moved when, after the long process of ritual robing, the crown was placed on her head. But she proceeds immediately to her chief support: 'My excellent Lord Melbourne, who stood very close to me throughout the whole ceremony, was completely overcome

The Queen liked dogs, and she liked people who liked dogs. Lord Melbourne qualified. Her terrier Islay, she reported, 'has a very odd trick of liking to lick and play with anything bright, and he remembers Lord M. giving him his glasses, and he sits begging before Lord M. the moment he sees them . . .'

at this moment, and very much affected; he gave me such a kind, and I may say *fatherly* look.' Victoria drew him bowing before her, touching her crown in the act of homage; and carrying the Sword of State, a majestic figure arrayed in scarlet and ermine. Benjamin Disraeli, watching the ceremony from the Commons' pews, observed that Melbourne carried the sword like a butcher, tripped over his robes and pitched his coronet over his nose. Lord Melbourne himself was so exhausted by the long ritual that he revived himself with a glass of wine off the altar in St Edward's chapel, on which, rather to Victoria's disapproval, sandwiches were also being served. But she had no word of reproach for Lord Melbourne's need, and when he complained he found the sword 'excessively heavy', she rejoined in sympathy that 'the Crown hurt me a good deal'.

Right: 'My kind Lord Melbourne', wrote the young Queen after her Coronation, 'was much affected in speaking of the whole ceremony.' He carried the Sword of State at the head of the solemn procession in the Abbey, and found it 'excessively heavy'.

Left: From her apartments in Buckingham Palace, Victoria could look across to Westminster Abbey, where her resplendent Coronation took place on 28 June 1838.

Lord Melbourne bearing the Sword.

She drew herself in the same album, a tiny figure viewed from the back, swamped in a mantle, and almost toppled by a disproportionately huge crown. It had been made specially for her, set with all the historic stones, to weigh much less — just over half — the ancient Crown of England, called St Edward's. It is interesting that Victoria, trained to notice details of braid and embroidery, pattern and cut in the costumes of ballet and opera, should show such rough disregard for the different robes that marked each stage of the sovereign's investment. She mentions them by name in her diary — the Dalmatic, the Supertunica of Cloth of Gold, the Purple Velvet Kirtle and Mantle — but indistinct scribble is all they merit in her drawings. The light slippers, just like

Wearing her circlet of diamonds, before the crowning, Victoria prayed. Her drawings of the ceremony are deeply serious — she recorded none of the mishaps and hitches and bewilderment that resulted from the lack of rehearsals.

Lady Fanny Cowper, daughter of Lord Melbourne's sister, was one of the eight trainbearers attending the Queen, with wreaths of silver corn and pink roses in their hair, and more roses on their silver and white satin dresses.

ballet shoes, embroidered with rosebuds and the royal arms in gold, and lined with white satin reading 'All Hail Victoria' in a wreath of rose, thistle and shamrock, are ignored; the richly ornate, bold brocade of her golden cope, also worked in the national symbols, is not even hinted at. She did take a little more trouble over her own face, showing how her hair was plaited and looped round her ears to show off their neatness.

P:V:del:K P. 1837. Count Waldstein.
from recollection.

Prince Esterhazy brought his 'good-looking' young compatriot Count Waldstein to visit Victoria's mother, to whom he was distantly related. Victoria enjoyed his conversation enormously, praising him as 'quiet, unassuming, sensible and highly talented'.

In spite of her attachment to Lord Melbourne, Victoria had eyes for others, and a number of much younger men saunter through the pages of her sketchbooks in a variety of fetching costumes. Under Melbourne's influence, she assumed publicly a certain cynicism towards marriage, but this did not prevent her recording possible candidates for her favour. Count Waldstein, bearded and romantically tousled, is drawn attractively. She met him at her eighteenth birthday party; but etiquette prevented her dancing with him, for 'he could not dance quadrilles', and Victoria was forbidden the valse or the gallop with a partner not of royal blood. Later Count Waldstein's 'pretty Hungarian uniform' and his striking accomplishments in art and music met with her approval. He gave her one of his paintings, of gipsies from his own country. She stuck it, of course, in an album.

The man who fascinated her so much that while at the opera she watched him rather than the stage was someone she had known as a child but never met again since — her cousin Charles, the Duke of Brunswick. Seeing him from a distance at a ball, Victoria was struck: 'He was in a black and dark blue uniform with silver; his hair hanging wildly about his face, his countenance pale and haggard; I was very sorry I could not see him de près for once.' The Duke had been declared unfit to rule; a coup of 1830 had placed his brother on the throne instead. 'I must say I think it was well felt in him not to come near', adds Victoria, a little uncertainly. 'En revanche his gentleman came very near, and I had a full view of him; he has nothing at all fierce or tigrish about him, except his long, (but *tidy*) hair.' She was obviously gripped when 'two ladies who have seen him [the Duke] at the balls tell me that when close by, his expression is dreadful, so very fierce and desperate . . . ' This saturnine desperado, this royal Heathcliff who so stirred Victoria's young curiosity, never regained his birthright; he became a collector of diamonds and died childless in Geneva in 1873.

Charles, the exiled Duke of Brunswick, mesmerized the young Queen. She quizzed him from her box at the opera and out riding in the park — 'He has a very fine, dark and stern countenance', she noted — and drew him (right) 'from recollection from a distance'. She sketched as well his companion the Count d'Anglau (above), 'also very handsome and wild-looking'.

The Queen was not entirely free to choose. Since her childhood Mama and Uncle Leopold, the shapers of her future, had planned — even schemed — that she should marry her first cousin, Prince Albert, the son of their brother Duke Ernest of Saxe-Coburg-Gotha. Both children had been brought up to expect it, but in July 1839, although Victoria remembered Albert with affection from his few days' visit in 1836, she wrote anxiously to Leopold, repudiating any idea that she had promised herself in marriage. After two years as an independent Queen Regnant, she thought she wanted to remain so.

It was therefore with feelings of hurt impatience that Prince Albert arrived at Windsor with his brother Ernest that winter. But the appearance of the man who loved music, and art and science as well as nightingales banished instantly all Victoria's reluctance and indifference. She stood at the top of the stairs at Windsor Castle to receive them, and immediately Albert stirred all her quick appreciativeness of good looks in men and all her ready, generous feelings: 'It was with some emotion that I beheld Albert — who is *beautiful*', she wrote in her diary. The next day she was enraptured by him: 'Albert really is quite charming, and so excessively handsome, such beautiful blue eyes, and exquisite nose, and such a pretty mouth with delicate moustachios and slight but very slight whiskers; a beautiful figure, broad in the shoulders and a fine waist.' She danced with him — he danced beautifully; she played Fox and Geese with him after dinner, and Tactics; they looked together at drawings by the Old Masters from her library.

The next day she told Melbourne — before she told Albert — that she had changed her mind, and wanted to marry. On 15 October, less than a week after Albert's arrival, she 'said to him, that I thought he must be aware *why* I wished them to come here — and that it would make me *too happy* if he would consent to what I wished . . . . I told him I was quite unworthy of him . . . I told him it was a great sacrifice — which he wouldn't allow . . . I feel the happiest of human beings.'

Leopold of Saxe-Coburg-Gotha, Victoria's uncle and later King of the Belgians, was her chief adviser and 'my real father, for I have none'.

They were both twenty, Albert the younger by just three months. The greatest difference between them was that Victoria had the unique psychological transparency that makes her diary such a compelling record of her life, while Albert was a closed character. In spite of a life of brilliant activity and splendid achievement, Albert remains a man across whom falls a shadow — the shadow of unlikeability. Yet he was a man of very fine quality, and Victoria's avowed inferiority complex beside him was well founded. In his twenties, before balding and thickening spoiled his appearance, he was indeed princely: tall, slender but strong, with the clear blue gaze of a Saxon and a romantic, well-cut profile, shapely hands, and long legs set off very well by the daring cut-away coats and tight breeches then in vogue. He was also able: well instructed, widely read, clever, filled with intellectual curiosity and the application to satisfy it. His education, devised by Leopold and the Coburg family shaman Baron Stockmar and supervised by their well-liked tutor Christoph Florschutz, took him to Brussels, Bonn and Rome and placed him in contact with such stimulating minds as Lambert Quételet the mathematician and Immanuel Fichte the philosopher.

Yet, for all his practical side, Albert was rather a dreamer, a man who gave way to stormy feelings at the piano or the organ (which he played well), who had a genuine collector's passion for art, not just the interest of conventional politesse. He was not easily approachable: Victoria, his elder daughters and a few intimates like Stockmar loved him, but in general he was admired and respected. The force of Victoria's love for him was such that perhaps she liked to have Albert this way, exclusively her own. But there is every indication that it did not make him happy. He was, in the double sense of the word, *étranger* — a foreigner, an outsider. He spoke excellent English, but German was his mother tongue. His combination of industry and sentiment, his persevering quest for moral improvement through art, reflected the highest philosophical ideals of German romanticism. Victoria, with her intuitive responses, saw in him this German atavism; her

Sir William Ross painted a miniature of Prince Albert for the Queen in the year of their engagement; she had it set in jewels and wore it as a bracelet all her life. This pencil sketch is an early copy of it.

favourite portrait of Albert, amongst very many that were painted, was by Robert Thorburn. At the Queen's request, he is dressed as a medieval Teutonic knight.

After the announcement of their engagement, Albert returned to Germany to say goodbye. He had a taste of his future wife's obstinacy when she appointed George Anson to be his Private Secretary, instead of someone of Albert's choice. Anson had occupied the same post on Lord Melbourne's staff, and Albert, who had pronounced ideas on the political neutrality of constitutional monarchy, did not want to be associated with Whiggery immediately he arrived in England. But Victoria would have her way, and Albert, on this occasion, acquiesced. There were other problems too. The Tories, angered by Victoria's open partisanship with the Whigs, reduced the customary grant of £50,000 a year for the Queen's husband to £30,000. But these trials became trifles when Albert returned and the couple were reunited: 'I embraced him now again, and he looked so dear and so well; seeing his *dear dear* face again put me at rest about everything!'

Albert was such a paragon of beauty in Victoria's eyes that she seems to have hesitated to sketch him, and these watercolours are the only portraits she made.

The profile (right) is again after Ross's miniature, and the full face (left) captures well Albert's serious idealism. At the top of the page we can see how she tried out her colours as she worked.

original Sketch by V R for the dress of the Queen's 12 Brides Maid

92

On 10 February 1840, in the Chapel Royal at St James's Palace, Victoria and Albert were married. She promised to obey him, though the Archbishop had asked her if she wanted the word deleted. After the ceremony, and the wedding breakfast, the couple drove to Windsor for a very short honeymoon — Victoria, robust in all things, and in defiance of Albert, wanted to get back to government as soon as possible. But all her fresh, happy, absolutely guileless immediacy is there on the pages of her diary. She describes how she had a headache after the long ordeal and retired to a sitting room, where she found Albert playing the piano. He took her on his knee and kissed her: 'I NEVER, NEVER spent such an evening!! My DEAREST DEAREST DEAR Albert sat on a footstool by my side and his excessive love and affection gave me feelings of heavenly love and happiness I never could have *hoped* to have felt before! He clasped me in his arms, and we kissed each other again and again! . . . to be called by names of tenderness, I have never heard used to me before — was bliss beyond belief! Oh! this was the happiest day of my life!'

Neither Victoria nor Albert came from a happy family. Albert's gentle and imaginative mother Louise had run away from her libertine husband and left her children when Albert was only five. He had never seen his mother again, but he bore her no grudge, indeed always spoke of her with understanding and tenderness. After his parents' divorce, his father Duke Ernest of Saxe-Coburg-Gotha married again; Albert and Victoria were both fond of Mama Marie, as they called her. Coburg had been for Albert 'a paradise', and there he had perfected his innate gift for amusing himself, hour after hour, without social stimulus except a single companion — formerly his much-loved brother Ernest, now his wife Victoria.

There began for the twenty-year-old Queen days of mutual activity and pleasure such as she had never known before. The isolation of her childhood was banished. Spicy conversations with Lord Melbourne continued, at least until he resigned in the following year; but with Albert there was

93

constant companionship, much less talking, and more doing. It is striking how very little Victoria quotes Albert's words. She gives his opinions, reactions, and state of mind, but his cadences are not audible, as Lord M.'s are. Yet the texture of their everyday existence, in the first year of their marriage, is palpable.

Albert, for all his goodness, was great fun to be with. On one of the first mornings she writes: 'Got up at 20 m. to 9. My dearest Albert put on my stockings for me. I went in and saw him shave; a great delight for me.' They spent their days walking, reading aloud to each other, looking at pictures, playing duets, accompanying the other singing. Albert's tastes predominated: the choice of literature was often Goethe — *Wilhelm Meister* — or Schiller, 'Das Lied von der Glocke'. The treasures of George III's collection at Windsor, hitherto largely unsorted and neglected, immediately fascinated him, and he began work on reorganizing the Royal Library. They still did the things Victoria had done before her marriage: there were dogs and horses and balls, but the

Victoria and Albert's first home was at Windsor Castle, which had been successfully restored, remodelled and redecorated in the romantic spirit of the Gothic revival by Jeffry Wyatville for Victoria's uncle George IV.

hours kept were earlier. In this she was pliant to him; but she did not yet let him see despatch boxes. To Victoria, Albert was a paragon, but to him Victoria was frustratingly authoritarian. 'I am only the husband, not the master', he complained.

Albert's education had been in every way more cosmopolitan and wide-ranging than Victoria's. This was true of his training in art. He drew with the intemperate earnestness that characterized so many of his enterprises: hussars, their uniforms accurately portrayed down to the last twist on the frogging, fill the pages of an album at Windsor which he completed before he was married. But his taste was formed, interesting and personal; he appreciated many painters, from Trecento Italians to contemporary masters such as the German portraitist Franz-Xavier Winterhalter, with a genuinely independent and knowledgeable eye. He was among the first to like and buy Italian primitives, and he encouraged

Victoria, whose natural taste, as displayed after Albert's death, was much less fine. Under his influence she bought a Lucas Cranach, for instance, as a Christmas present for him in the first year of their marriage, and over the years she presented him with several masterpieces — some Cima da Conegliano panels, and Bernardo Daddi's magnificent *Marriage of the Virgin*.

Prince Albert did not reject the contemporary painters Victoria had patronized before their marriage: Edwin Landseer, whom she had commissioned to paint her favourite dogs, and George Hayter, who had painted her as a girl and whom she appointed 'my Painter of History and Portrait' four days after her accession. After her marriage both artists were invited to Court, to coach the young couple in a medium that had taken Albert's fancy, for it ideally combined science and art: etching. In the autumn of 1840, a copperplate printing press was set up in Buckingham Palace by the master-printers Richard Holdgate and Henry Graves. Victoria was expecting her first child, and she passed her days quietly, resting a great deal, listening to her husband reading, and etching — sometimes from her own work, sometimes from sketches by Albert. Often they worked together. She traced the compositions and then transferred them with a needle on to the wax, gum and pitch preparation on the plate. Etching suited her light, rapid eye, and though the early results are sometimes a little stiff and insipid, the later etchings of dogs and children are much more lively and full of charm. Underneath she always inscribed, sometimes forgetting to invert the lettering and so avoid the mirror effect of printing — *VR del. et sclt.*, *Albert del. VR sclt.*, or *VR del. et A. sclt.*

Etching relaxed her: 'We spent a delightful, peaceful morning — singing after breakfast, and etching together', she wrote after their first attempt. Hayter was present to give advice; under his supervision Victoria copied a turbaned head by Stefano della Bella, a seventeenth-century Florentine artist well represented in the Royal Collection. Amazingly, this is the only artist whom Victoria ever copied who was not a contemporary or near contemporary. She preferred

Victoria's terrier Islay, engraved by her (above) and by her master Edwin Landseer (below).

Right: A copy, etched by Victoria, of a drawing by the seventeenth-century Florentine, Stefano della Bella.

Her Majesty Queen Victoria's first etching

G. Hayter

Augᵗ 29. 1840.
Windsor Castle

modern work, and from Hayter's own vast output she chose to copy on to a plate his profile head of her husband from the big tableau he painted of their wedding.

Victoria was not at this stage as intolerant as she became in later years. She admired Hayter's virtuosity — he was famous for producing 189 likenesses in his monumental history painting *The Trial of Queen Caroline* — and over-looked his private affairs. She told Lord Melbourne that she knew Hayter had not been elected to the Royal Academy because 'he had quarrelled with his wife, and had separated from her. "And did he get another?" said Lord M. I laughed and said I was not sure of that.' So little did Victoria mind the irregularity, she knighted him in 1842.

Landseer's art was of a different order. As a child he had kept carcasses of animals hidden under his bed so that he could study their anatomy at night. His animal painting was often vigorous and masterly, but occasionally sentimentally anthropomorphized. This appealed hugely to Victoria, as did his rough, nearly risqué sense of humour. She thought him 'certainly the cleverest artist there is', and examining his work through a magnifying glass, could not get over his

Albert and Victoria worked side by side at their etching plates, sometimes collaborating on the same drawing. Albert corrected his wife's efforts, and encouraged her to annotate in detail. As her skill grew, she began to draw directly on to the plate, as with the washerwoman and the man in a fez in this etching of 1843.

In May 1842 James Planché was commissioned to dress Victoria and Albert as Edward III and Philippa for a ball to raise funds for the silk workers of Spitalfields. The Queen added these 'rough sketches' to her diary, and then asked Edwin Landseer to commemorate the costumes in a monumental portrait.

exquisite handling of detail. They made friends, and she and Albert when out riding together in London would sometimes call on the painter in his studio to look at his latest work, or help him with an impromptu sitting for one of their numerous commissions.

In May 1842, Victoria and Albert posed for Landseer in the costumes of Queen Philippa and Edward III, which had been designed for them by the theatrical designer Planché for a special ball at Buckingham Palace. Albert, who always hoped to turn even frivolity to good, wanted to raise money for the unemployed Spitalfields weavers and therefore commanded all the guests to dress in silk. But it was a misguided gesture: his philanthropic energies needed a larger scale of operation. They were soon to receive it.

Pussy.

Before going to Bed.

By late 1842 Albert was effectively acting as the Queen's Private Secretary. He was reading state papers, commenting, drafting memoranda and guiding her. His ascendancy was achieved by a combination of diplomacy, strength of mind and chance, and his influence was healing, both to Victoria herself and to the country he had adopted.

Chance played its part because Victoria was weakened by pregnancy and childbirth. The Princess Royal was born so soon — 21 November 1840 — that she must have been conceived in the very first weeks of their marriage. This was bad luck and Victoria felt it keenly, especially after the 'good many hours suffering' she endured during the birth. Victoria and Albert both adored 'Pussy', as Vicky was first known, and Victoria filled her diary with comments and her albums with drawings and etchings of the Pussette's cleverness and beauty. But it was a terrible blow when she found that she was immediately pregnant again. This pregnancy made her

'Pussy' was the nickname of the Princess Royal, Victoria, etched here by her mother as she is washed in the royal nursery.

Victoria was at her best drawing spontaneously scenes from her immediate and personal surroundings, like this sketch of Vicky on gold-crested writing paper.

feel 'quite done up', 'very wretched', 'tired and depressed' and 'very low'. She was barely twenty-one, had been married under two years, and was having her second child. Even the birth of a longed-for Prince of Wales on 9 November 1841, within a year of Vicky, did not raise her from her lassitude. Albert was astonished to find that, while he was reading summaries of important papers to her on Parliamentary debates, she fell asleep. He had had the keys of the despatch boxes during her confinement with Vicky; after the birth of the Prince of Wales he did not have to give them back. She wrote of Bertie's birth afterwards: 'My sufferings were really very severe, and I don't know what I should have done, but for the great comfort and support my beloved Albert was to me during the whole time.'

At the side of his wife in childbirth, Albert was allowed the role of protector, colleague, minister, mentor, doctor and lover that he had desired to play from the beginning. His usefulness was now assured: at home, he had reconciled Victoria with her mother whom she had since her accession cruelly cold-shouldered, and he had finally persuaded his wife to wean herself from Lehzen, who through jealousy and insecurity had created much mischief between them since their marriage. In September 1842 the governess left for Germany, and though Victoria had seemed to cling to her, the parting was accomplished so easily that it must have been a relief. In politics, Albert had quickly forged strong links with Lord Melbourne's successor as Prime Minister, the Tory Sir Robert Peel, an active reformer after Albert's heart. In the country as a whole, Albert had won a notable mark of confidence when, during the Queen's first confinement, he was appointed sole Regent in the event of her death.

Victoria's moorings to the past were cast off: Albert filled all her present and her future. As Greville noted with his usual dyspepsia: 'He is really discharging the functions of the Sovereign. He is King to all intents and purposes.'

Beatrice

By Osborne March 12 1860

FOUR

Scenes from Family Life

Victoria did not enjoy submitting, but she accepted submission as woman's lot with a completeness that amounted to an endorsement. The early meetings for women's suffrage enraged her. She wanted 'this mad, wicked folly of "Woman's Rights"' checked immediately, and thought one of the leaders should be whipped; the whole subject made 'the Queen', she wrote, 'so furious that she cannot contain herself.' Yet she did kick against the pricks, complaining to her daughter Vicky: 'There is great happiness and great blessedness in devoting oneself to another who is worthy of one's affection; still men are very selfish and the woman's devotion is always one of submission which makes our poor sex so very unenviable.'

Beatrice was the youngest of Victoria and Albert's nine children. The Queen liked sketching her children from the back and picking out such details as the big bow and lacy washable dress-saver Beatrice is wearing over her fashionable purple frock.

The aspect of womanhood that especially moved Queen Victoria's sympathy was childbearing. She herself was wonderfully strong and healthy, and gave birth, without physical complications, to nine children in seventeen years, of whom only one — the youngest son Leopold, born in 1853 — suffered from any innate ailment. (He was a haemophiliac, and died at the age of thirty-one.) Victoria's is a formidable record of maternity, and unrepresentative of the

103

time, when death from puerperal fever was commonplace and infant mortality high. She was aware that she had been more fortunate than many women: 'Few were or are better than I was', she wrote, not in a tone of pride, but of compassion. But in a telling image she called maternity 'the shadow side' of life.

In a letter to Vicky soon after her daughter's marriage in 1858, she revealed some of the strain her enormous family had cost her: 'Now to reply to your observation that you find a married woman has much more liberty than an unmarried one; in one sense of the word she has, — but what I meant was — in a physical point of view — and if you have hereafter (as I had constantly for the first 2 years of my marriage) — aches — and sufferings and miseries and plagues — which you must struggle against — and enjoyments etc. to give up — constant precautions to take, you will feel the yoke of a married woman! . . . I had 9 times for 8 months to bear with those abovenamed enemies and real misery, (besides many duties) and I own it tried me sorely; one feels so pinned down — one's wings clipped . . . only half oneself . . . And therefore, I think our sex a most unenviable one.'

Right: Vicky, the firstborn, made quick progress: at about the time of this pen and ink sketch, Vicky was reading 'before me, and so nicely'. The toy pram she is pushing was an innovation: the 'perambulator' itself was a very recent Victorian product.

Alfred & Alice

Queen Victoria had all her children at home, either at Buckingham Palace or Windsor Castle. The Queen's Physician Accoucher was in attendance at each birth and the same monthly nurse, Mrs Lilly, assisted her throughout all nine confinements. The Queen trusted her: 'she is an excellent, clever, sensible woman, and still very handy and quick in what she does . . . ' Victoria was always pleased to see her go, however, because she was then 'émancipé', and 'so glad and thankful to be able now quite to resume my normal life', her old pastimes and her work. But the person who made her

Prince Alfred — pictured here with Princess Alice, his elder by only fifteen months — was very attached to his sister, and when she married he wept bitterly.

Alice
April 25 - 1845.

On her second birthday Alice, garlanded in flowers and dressed in a new spring frock, came down before dinner to receive and give her presents.

sufferings tolerable was Albert. Contrary to our prejudice about Victorian prudery, the Prince was present at Queen Victoria's side almost all the time, there remaining to lift and carry and comfort and help, to read and sing and summarize despatches and deal with visitors throughout the fortnight or more after the birth when Victoria, like all prosperous women of her time, remained in bed. He is 'so wonderfully handy and gentle', wrote Victoria gratefully. When the Archbishop of Canterbury and other dignitaries, whose presence was customary as witnesses to royal births, missed

Princess Alice's entry, Albert in his thoughtfulness took the opportunity to change this intrusive practice.

The Duchess of Kent had nursed Victoria herself, unlike her first children Feodore and Charles. Breastfeeding was considered unusual for a lady at the time. By the 1840s, however, all manuals advocated it, and the practice was spreading to the aristocracy. Victoria, who found it horribly indelicate when someone spoke of morning sickness at dinner, does not say in her diary whether she would have liked to nurse her own children. Her duties as a reigning queen would have made it difficult, but her horror of 'animal-like' biology probably made it repugnant to her anyway. Later, she advised her daughter Vicky not to breastfeed, warning her against indulging in 'Baby-worship' or overdoing 'the passion for the nursery'.

The glorious assemblies of Victoria's progeny, painted in a rich palette borrowed from High Renaissance celebrations of the blessed gathered in heaven, or of heroes and poets on Parnassus, have accustomed us to forget 'the shadow side'. Nor did Queen Victoria herself want it commemorated or recorded. The idyll of family happinesses that filled album after album, inspiring watercolours, miniatures, photographs and her own drawings, disguise it. Such a pictorial chronicle was a Victorian family obsession, and in this respect as in so many others Victoria and Albert and their children provide a microcosm of the prevailing ethic, accurately reflecting the society over which they reigned.

For in spite of Queen Victoria's disgust, it would be quite wrong to impute to her any resentment towards her children. She was a committed, conscientious and loving mother. Her overflowing sentiments of motherly attachment and her real pleasure in her children's natures, appearances, activities, progress and company typify the new parental response that developed towards the end of the eighteenth century, when the child was consecrated the symbol of goodness and purity in such influential works as Rousseau's treatise on education, *Emile*, or the novels of Dickens.

Right: With a bold use of cross-hatching, a result of her interest in etching at this date, the Queen sketched Princess Alice with her nurse in the grounds of Buckingham Palace.

Overleaf: The brilliant use of colour, the assured evocation of pleasant heat, the firmly handled idyllic atmosphere in this family scene at Osborne House in 1850 show the influence of William Leighton Leitch, a master watercolourist who started teaching the Queen in 1842 and continued to visit her regularly at all her houses.

Left: Franz-Xavier Winterhalter was Victoria and Albert's most admired portrait painter, and in 1846 he produced an opulent canvas of the royal couple enthroned with their first five children around them. The Queen made this quick ink sketch of the composition.

A conversazione group, like the famous Winterhalter portrait of 1846 showing Victoria and Albert enthroned side by side, with the first five children — Vicky, Bertie, Alice and Alfred — gathered like secular seraphim attendant on the Holy Family around their parents and the newborn Princess Helena, presents a new and determined argument about the nature of domestic life. Victoria loved this picture, and copied its superb stylish composition in a quick pen and ink sketch. It was in her opinion 'one of the finest modern pictures painted . . . in the style of a Paul Veronese . . . ' Prince Albert instructed the artist to paint 'fine turquoise-blue skies' in the background, enhancing the atmosphere of sublime content breathed by the whole picture.

Although Queen Victoria herself rarely painted in a background to the portraits of her children that from 1840 onwards began to flow from her pen and her brush, her visual language is as unclouded and serene as Winterhalter's. In the thick morocco-bound volume, stamped in gold 'Sketches of the Royal Children by V.R. from 1841–59,' she pasted dozens of watercolours and drawings of her offspring, annotating them with captions such as 'Pussy with Bertie in

Right: Both these drawings of Vicky were made when the Queen was absorbed with etching, and she later engraved them and gave prints to her friends. Eos the greyhound, pictured here with the two-year-old Vicky, was the Prince Consort's favourite dog. He brought her from Coburg, and when she died he had her statue placed on the sculpture terrace at Osborne, where it is today.

Viley — Claremont Jan: 15 — 43

Viley & as — Jan: 15th 1843
193. — Claremont

the dresses they wore on little Alice's christening day June 2 1843'. Pussy absorbed her mother more than any of the subsequent children. She is sketched crawling, being bathed by her nurse, taking her bottle and showing the first signs of interest in the external world — in a coloured ball, in a caged bird. The other children usually graduated into the family album as toddlers, planted foursquare on sturdy legs under flounces and petticoats. Their dress — frocks were worn by the boys as well until the age of five or thereabouts — is painted with pride: the plaid silks, trimmed bonnets, gorgeous sashes, satin bows on sleeves and frills threaded with ribbon, the pleats and tucks on clothes which were, in a house where profligacy was frowned on, handed down from one child to another. Interest in costume dominates; the Queen had a preference for back views. Though she was good at likenesses, they were perhaps an effort: she often copied the faces from Sir William Ross's miniatures.

Right: Until they were five or six, Victorian children of both sexes wore dresses, the only difference being that the girls' skirts were gored while those of the boys, like Arthur's pictured here, were pleated.

Below: On New Year's Day 1844, Vicky, aged three, was dressed up in a blue and white silk dress copied from a West portrait of Princess Charlotte.

Arthur

VR. del. May 7 - 1853
Osborne.

Bertie
Ve del Ballon
Voice
Sept: 16. 185[...]

116

Concealment was not Queen Victoria's forte, and the determined rhetoric of a family idyll in her album does not hide her preferences and disappointments. Pussy is the heroine; Bertie, the Prince of Wales, begins well, with loving drawings of his infant progress, playing with Vicky, or with a rabbit, or with the parrots that the Queen had always enjoyed as pets. But after the age of ten Bertie disappears from the album, except in family groups. She had set great store by 'Albert junior's likeness to dearest papa', but it seemed to fade as Bertie, unlike his clever elder sister, failed to take to his lessons. 'There is much good in him', sighed his mother on his ninth birthday. 'He has such affectionate feelings, — great truthfulness and great simplicity of character'. But Mr Gibbs, the tutor engaged for the Prince of Wales, was a typically serious choice of the Prince Consort. His academic sobriety and his rigorous discipline were

Victoria, Albert, Alfred, Alice.

My own from nature.
July 1846.

quite unsuited to the child's nature. Bertie was difficult: 'A very bad day', reported Mr Gibbs on 8 March 1852. 'The P. of W. has been like a person half silly. I could not gain his attention. He was very rude, particularly in the afternoon, throwing stones in my face. . . . He made faces and spat. . . . There was a great deal of bad words'. Prince Albert, taking up one of his pseudo-scientific hobbies, had the bumps of his elder children read by the leading phrenologist, Dr George Combe. The sage pronounced Bertie's bumps of 'combative-ness' and 'destructiveness' and 'ostentativeness' very large. But Vicky's cleverness was obvious, right down to the last bump, and favouritism was one of her parents' failings. It is no wonder that Bertie, when he was informed that he would succeed to the throne, was sadly puzzled that he should take precedence over Vicky.

Many of Victoria's paintings of her children, like the portrait of Princess Alice (above), show the influence of Sir William Ross.

The picture of her two elder daughters (above right), begun in May 1846, was interrupted by the birth of Princess Helena, painted (right) in the local peasant costume of Albert's Gotha homeland.

Alice & Vicky begun Aug & finished Nov: 1846.
V. R.

Leuchow (Helena)

Prince Arthur, the third son, was Victoria's favourite child, and inspired this rare nude study (left). He was born on 1 May 1850, the eighty-first birthday of the 'beloved hero' the Duke of Wellington, after whom he was named. He is pictured below, aged four, in the uniform of the Grenadier Guards.

Arthur — May 17 1853 —

Arthur. —

The Queen's love of good looks influenced her attitude to her children: she hated Bertie's knock-knees and the largeness of his features, especially his long Hanoverian nose 'which begins to hang a little'. There is hardly a single drawing of Leopold on his own, though his brothers, especially the blue-eyed, graceful Arthur, inspired his mother's pen to chronicle their growth. Leopold 'is a very common-looking child, very plain in the face', wrote his mother; 'clever but an oddity — and not an engaging child though amusing.' Arthur on the other hand was 'a precious love', and though Victoria was of the opinion that 'the prettiest [child] is frightful when undressed', she painted Arthur naked, like an Italian *putto*. Beatrice, the last of all, and always affectionately called Baby, delighted her mother. She was the second child to be born under 'soothing, quieting and delightful' chloroform. Baby 'is such a pretty, plump, flourishing child . . .' wrote Victoria, 'with fine large blue eyes, marked nose, pretty little mouth and very fine skin.'

Prince Leopold, fourth and last of Victoria and Albert's sons, suffered from haemophilia, endemic in the next generation of the family. This sketch of him playing with Arthur is one of the very few drawings of Leopold made by his mother.

a)

b)

Baby Beatrice was the favourite daughter, and she grew even closer to her mother after the death of Prince Albert when she was four. The Queen almost abandoned painting her family during her widowhood, but she made an exception for Beatrice's blonde-red head.

Victoria was not alone in adoring her children; Albert led the way. In 1842, he had himself drawn in pastel by Landseer as a present for the Queen on his own birthday: he gazes down into the small round face of the Princess Royal whom he holds in his arms. The assignment of baby love to female psychology is a later social phenomenon: to the Prince Consort babies seemed a natural spur to pride and interest and love, as much in the father as in the mother. The Queen records in her diary the precious times they enjoyed with Vicky in the morning and afternoon, how they would visit the nursery twice a day or how Vicky would be brought down to see them. Albert is always very much in evidence in these diary entries, especially about Vicky. She was the firstborn, beloved for that alone, but she remained her father's favourite always on account of her aptitude, quickness, forwardness and talents. Albert's joy in her leaps from his wife's pages: the young father trundling his daughter about in 'that basket, or go-cart, which came from Paris', or setting her on his knee to 'touch the keys of the piano, which delighted her'.

In 1849 James Izzard, Turner in Ordinary to Her Majesty and the Royal Family, charged the nursery 12/6 for repairing a 'Skin Horse' and providing a new mane and tail and bridle and saddle.

124

Albert also took on more serious responsibilities for his children's upbringing. He had a broad sense of family life, and he became the architect for the royal household's totally novel style. From 1842 onwards, he purged the staff: Lehzen was not the only person to go. Mrs Southey, sister-in-law of the poet, was dismissed from her post as Superintendent of the Nursery and was replaced, until 1851, by 'Laddle', the efficient Lady Lyttelton. A heavy 'Plan' of lessons was devised for the children and their tutors. Queen Victoria herself undertook Vicky's religious instruction, in the evenings, a privilege that made the excluded Bertie somewhat wistful. As the children grew up, Papa spent an hour a day instructing them himself, adding this duty to his already crammed timetable. For all his commitment to improving pursuits, Albert was an inventive father, and liked having 'our tribe' about him. He took them to the theatre, to see the waxworks at Madame Tussaud's, and to visit the new animals at the Zoo, a recently founded institution that much appealed to the Prince Consort's scientific bent. But the greatest monument to Albert and Victoria's pioneering of the modern nuclear family was the building of Osborne House, the royal retreat on the Isle of Wight.

125

Osborne House, which Victoria and Albert made their family home for the summers, was set in extensive acres of good farmland. The annual haymaking was always a great event: Albert turned somersaults in the stacks to show Bertie how to do them. But the Prince Consort's farming interests were also more serious: he built model workers' cottages on the estate and designed a complex and innovatory drainage system.

The accommodation at all the royal houses, their lack of comforts, hygiene and conveniences, and the appalling cumbrousness of their administrative structure, horrified the young Prince when he first came to live at Windsor and at Buckingham Palace. When the Queen was lying in after the birth of the Princess Royal, Mrs Lilly heard a sound in her room. Under the sofa, a small boy was found: he had visited the royal apartments, he admitted, secretly and without hindrance on a number of occasions, had sat on the Queen's throne and heard the new-born princess squall. Such slackness affronted the deepest parts of Albert's clear and organized mind. He prised retainers out of ancient sinecures and streamlined the staff, offending many but achieving order.

Even so Albert had an urgent need for home life, deriving from Coburg well-being, that was hitherto unknown in the house of the English royal family, and it was soon clear that neither Windsor nor Buckingham Palace, let alone the exotic Brighton Pavilion, provided the fast increasing family with a home.

The Isle of Wight was easy of access from the capital, yet distant enough to give the needed sense of release from state affairs. Victoria had liked it when she stayed at Norris Castle as a girl in 1833. In 1845 she bought, out of her own income (she was much more thrifty than her uncles), Osborne House, set in good farmland on a rise above the Solent, cradled by slopes and rolling hay fields, yet on a sufficient crest to give breathtakingly beautiful views over the Solent. The pleased Queen wrote to her uncle: 'It sounds so snug and nice to have a place of *one's own*, quiet and retired, and free from all . . . other charming Departments who really are the plague of one's life.'

When the Queen was at Osborne, she relaxed. The splendid situation above the Solent created a peaceful, holiday atmosphere, and the weather, judging from her Journal and her watercolours, seems always to have been fine.

Prince Albert, masterful and energetic as ever, immediately laid plans: the old house was to be pulled down and a new house, built with every contemporary invention, to rise in its place. With characteristic independence of spirit, he overlooked all architects and chose instead the master builder whose sweeping reconstruction of Belgravia had much impressed him: Thomas Cubitt, who liked and understood up to date methods as much as the Prince.

Together, they designed Osborne House. On a series of massive ornamental terraces facing the sea, a stucco'd villa began to take form, with an Italian campanile-style flag tower on one wing — the Pavilion — and another, differently scaled clock tower standing at an angle to it over the Household quarters. The asymmetrical profile and determined vernacular rather than palatial appearance of the building was bold and successful, and very attractive. Above

One of the delights of the Isle of Wight was sea-bathing. From a bathing-house such as this, on the beach below Norris Castle close to Osborne, Victoria would step into a bathing machine which was then drawn down into the sea by a horse.

This painting of the new Pavilion wing at Osborne shows Edward Lear's influence in the strongly inked outlines, the fluidity of the strokes, the attention to architectural detail. With a touch of pride, Victoria adds to the watercolour that it was only partly copied from Lear.

all, Osborne was a superbly conceived home, which is what Albert wanted for his wife and his children. In the Pavilion wing, he and Victoria had a set of rooms, ample yet enfolding, with magnificent bow windows giving flowing views of the sea. Their rooms are arranged *en suite*, in a horseshoe shape with no corridor, so conveniently intimate; the technology of the 1840s assured them the hitherto unknown luxury of running hot water in baths that were plumbed in to drain as well. Above these private rooms was situated the nursery, so that the parents could make their cherished visits to the children with ease; below were the official audience and reception rooms. Even these have a cosy Biedermeier-like atmosphere, with the statues by Mary Thornycroft of the children dressed as Thomson's The Seasons, the deeply cushioned sofas, and the drapes.

As the children grew up, they moved away from their parents and across to another wing, nearer to the staff Household wing. This was connected to the Pavilion by an open arcaded passageway that was not only decorative and original, but effectively cut off both geographically and psychologically the staff from the family and sealed the latter's domestic happiness together more completely.

129

Albert planted drifts of dark-leaved bushes against the brightness of the wide lawns, and rare trees in groups about the grounds; he designed alcoves, much loved by Victoria, to provide shelter in which to draw and read and write, amongst formal terraces of flowerbeds set off by statues. In the house itself, the royal collection of contemporary painting and furniture — few pieces at Osborne were made earlier than 1826 — created an opulent, but utterly unforbidding interior. Albert and Victoria's taste was remarkably voluptuous: *Florinda*, which used to hang in Victoria's sitting room opposite the two desks at which she and Albert worked side by side, abounds with glabrous nudes rendered by Winterhalter in his most lacquered yet luscious manner. Victoria gave it to Albert for his birthday in 1852, and they both remarked how like a German relation of theirs was one of the frolicking nymphs.

Thomas Cubitt's bold and original plan of two dissimilar but balancing towers gave Osborne House a famous profile, copied in holiday houses from England to the United States. Victoria's sweeping watercolour shows how her handling of shadows was being developed by her teachers, but perspective still caused her problems.

In July 1849 a 'rustic fête' was held at Barton Farm, one of Osborne's dependencies, to celebrate the hay harvest. Victoria painted the gay tents, where after a hands' dinner, sailors and neighbours joined in to play 'Blindman's Buff, Leapfrog, Cricket...' and dance the Hornpipe.

The children were not forgotten. In 1853, Albert imported a Swiss chalet, one of the first prefabricated buildings to be assembled in England, and equipped it with a kitchen for the children to learn cooking, allotments for each of them to learn gardening, and a most contemporary model of a fort — no crusader romance or sandcastle nostalgia here — for the royal war games. They went on boating expeditions with their parents, and the family's deep content colours many pages of the Queen's diary. In August 1857, she described a typical day: 'Very hot and perfectly still . . . in the afternoon embarked in the Fairy with the 6 eldest children, Ladies &c and steamed to Sconie[?] Point and back. Beautiful calm evening and the sea like oil. Home late. We dined alone with Vicky, and afterwards went out on the Terrace and watched falling stars. Splendid reflection of the moon in the sea. Reading and playing.'

Bertie & Lenchen — Jan: 1 · 1851 ___ Alfred & Louise

Each of their birthdays, and important anniversaries like that of their parents' wedding, were ritually celebrated: birthday tables decorated with swags and wreaths were laden with presents, plays were performed, concerts were given, fancy dresses made and worn. At Victoria's thirty-fifth birthday party, all the children contributed, Princess Louise, then aged six, ending the evening with a grand solo performance of a 'Scale in C'. There was an edifying side: part of Racine's *Athalie* was acted in French; plays like A.F.F. von Kotzebue's *Das Hahnenschlag* (The Cockshy), a gentle bucolic piece, gave a polish to their German.

This harmony is the substance of Victoria's drawings of her growing family during her twenties and thirties. What astonishes the spectator today is that its motive force and inspiration, Prince Albert, is invisible. The Queen never drew or painted her husband with her children. He is absent. The unflagging work he undertook, both on his own account and on the Queen's, passes unrecorded. Victoria's subject matter, it is true, did not encompass politics, but it is very surprising not to find Albert the paterfamilias at all in her albums. It is equally conspicuous that after Albert's death

Minerva

Beatrice — Victoria — Alice — Leopold — Alfred.

The first five children wear the costume of Thuringian peasants to mark an occasion — but in an unusual oversight, the Queen did not date this lively sketch.

Victoria's interest in the family lost its liveliness. The album of 'Sketches of the Royal Children' is stamped Volume One, but the entries end in 1861, when the Prince Consort died; blank pages only remain, with here and there a loose sketch thrown in, but not pasted down. There is no second volume. Yet the much-loved Beatrice was still only four years old. The camera was of course replacing the pencil, and Victoria was an avid collector of photographs. It seems nevertheless that Albert gave her the incentive to paint her children — that she did this, as she did so much else, because he liked it. The imagery of family pleasure was not exactly hollow for her, but it was borrowed, and she needed Albert beside her to mastermind it. On one of their rare separations, in 1857, when Albert went to Belgium for the wedding of King Leopold's daughter, Charlotte, Victoria wrote to her uncle to congratulate him, and in a revealing passage added: 'you cannot think *combien cela me coûte* or how completely *déroutée* I am and *feel* when he is away, or how I count the hours till he returns. *All* the numerous children are as *nothing* to me when *he is away*; it seems as if the whole life of the house and home were gone, when he is away!'

The interplay of personal inclination and social ethos is always very complex. Queen Victoria mirrored her times' discovery of the family as the fountainhead of happiness and the microcosm of a happy society, she reflected its concern with material comforts and prosperity as the reward of virtue and endeavour. She herself was very proud of her family in this respect: as early as 1844, then the mother of only three children, she wrote: 'They say no Sovereign was ever more loved than I am (I am bold enough to say), & *this* because of our domestic home, the good example it presents.' But her satisfaction with the children was derived from Albert: the

Right: When she was thirteen, the Princess Royal came down to a formal dinner with her parents for the first time.

Below: A small theatre was specially built at Windsor for the frequent family theatricals. The Queen painted this scene from a German play, Die Tafelbirnen, *put on for Victoria and Albert's thirteenth wedding anniversary.*

Feb:10 . 1853

Helena — Alice Alfred Scene from the Play of Die Tafel Birnen
Louise   Bertie . Vicky —

My del May 21—

Vicky in her 1st Drawing room dress
May 20 - 1854.

Just before her twenty-sixth birthday, Victoria drew this image of unflinching self-scrutiny. After eight years of ruling, the face in the mirror is that of a serious, obstinate young woman, a little overwhelmed at the speed and weight of events, and determined not to show it, not to yield.

pleasure he took in fatherhood, and the moral and philosophical stress he laid upon it.

The matriarchal image posterity has made of the Queen, though it accurately reflects her strength, her imperiousness and her will, distorts the truth of her own idea of herself and her absolute adherence to the idea of patriarchy. For in her own eyes, her position as Queen Regnant was 'anomalous': 'It is a reversal of the right order of things which distressed me much and which no one, but such a perfection, such an angel as [Albert] is — could bear and carry through.' Fortunately, however hard she schooled herself in adoration and abnegation, her natural spirit did not bend altogether, and some of the family pleasure — and pain — originated with her.

Woman & Child
Cherbourg —
(from recollection) Aug. 18. 1857.

Woman at Bricquebec
Normandy
Aug. 18. 1857.

FIVE

Travels Abroad

*All the women', noted the Queen on a trip to Cherbourg in the summer of 1857, 'wear caps, many the regular Cauchaine ones, and full woollen skirts, with aprons and fichus ...' She took with enthusiasm to travelling, relishing different, unfamiliar customs.

Queen Victoria, ruling over the Empire at the time of its greatest expansion, never saw any of her dominions beyond the British Isles. Yet ever since she had glimpsed at St Leonards sailors from Spain lounging on the quay, and young fisher boys in clogs from Normandy, anything and especially anyone foreign seemed to her captivatingly exotic. At a time when the art of engraving was bringing before people's eyes for the first time the beauties and wonders of 'abroad', Victoria was an eager consumer of travellers' tales. The splendours of the Alhambra described by Washington Irving, the Oriental Tableaux drawn by Lady Wilhelmina Stanhope — a friend and one of her trainbearers at the Coronation — *Sketches of Persia* by an anonymous 'Traveller', all these excited her, even though she felt such 'Arabian-like tales' were not quite respectable. She had come across Edward Lear, not as a composer of nonsense songs but as a recorder of delightful excursions in Italy and elsewhere.

It was not the custom for the monarch to go abroad. Of her immediate predecessors, only George IV had done so, to visit his own kingdom of Hanover. The last English ruler to see Paris was Henry VI, when he was crowned King of France in Notre Dame in 1431; the last to set foot in France had been Henry VIII, on the Field of the Cloth of Gold. But faster communications made it possible for the monarch to leave the country and yet remain in contact, and Victoria was delighted that she did not have to appoint a Regent in her absence, as had been the practice until then. She thus pioneered both the regal tradition of grand diplomatic travel, and incognito royal holidays.

Victoria was twenty-four before she left the British Isles. The nation had presented her with a superb yacht, the *Victoria and Albert*, a paddle steamer carrying sail as well, so large and luxurious that even the Emperor Napoleon III, no stinter himself, observed when he saw it that he should like

This view of Portland, painted from the deck of the Victoria and Albert *on one of the family's sailing trips from the Isle of Wight, shows again in its deft penmanship the inspiring influence of Edward Lear, who had tutored Victoria the month before.*

one like it, but smaller. In 1843 the Queen and Prince Albert, leaving behind Vicky and Bertie as well as the new baby Alice, sailed across the Channel; breaking the coldness of centuries, they were to visit the King of the French, Louis Philippe, *en famille* in his castle of Eu in Normandy.

The *Victoria and Albert* outdistanced the naval escort, and her passengers were soon 'horrified not to know *where* we were'. But the Prince de Joinville, one of Louis Philippe's sons, found them and came on board to greet them, so early that Victoria was not even dressed They proceeded along the Normandy coast, and the Queen became very nervous as the moment of arrival in France drew near: 'at length Joinville discerned the King's barge approaching and as it came nearer and nearer, I felt still more agitated.' She nearly cried, she wrote, when Louis Philippe, all impatience, clambered on board and kissed her warmly.

The Queen found the French countryside pretty, 'enhanced by the setting sun', but was particularly delighted to note the 'crowds of people (all so different to ours)' and the 'number of Troops (also so different to our Troops)'. The strangeness continued to fill her with enthusiasm: the gardeners working beneath her windows — on a Sunday; the

When the Queen visited Louis Philippe at his Normandy home of Château d'Eu, the King organized a military band to play for them daily: 'The Band of the 24th Regiment (Infantry) (légère) played under my window, and extremely well', she wrote, but she found French soldiers 'so different to ours; very military looking, but little men.'

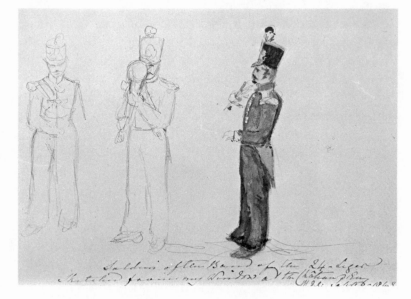

'faces, dress, manners, everything . . . so extremely different';
the swaddled babies and the tall white caps of the women; the
Catholic paraphernalia of wayside crucifixions and 'bijou'
chapels; and the French King and Queen's private chara-
bancs, which transported the huge royal party on *fêtes
champêtres* in the grounds, and which Albert later copied to
accommodate his growing family at Osborne. 'I felt as
though it were a dream', sighed Victoria, 'that I was at Eu,
and that my favourite Air Castle of so *many* years should at
length be realised.'

Though Eu was palatial, the style of the Citizen King had
the same personal, family quality so prized by Victoria and
Albert. Louis Philippe and his Queen, the Bourbon Marie-
Amélie, were surrounded by their children and their
children's children, and Victoria was radiant at the huge long
family breakfasts. The King's 'liveliness & vivacity & little
impatiences are my great delight and amusement . . . ' she
wrote. The Orléans and the Coburgs were intertwined by
any number of marriages — Louis Philippe's daughter Louise
was Uncle Leopold's wife, who gave Victoria motherly
advice as well as gowns in the latest Parisian fashion; his son
the Duke of Nemours was married to Victoire, daughter of
Victoria and Albert's uncle Ferdinand of Saxe-Coburg-
Gotha, and the beautiful childhood playmate of Albert,
whom he at one time thought of marrying. In spite of this,
Victoire de Nemours was one of Queen Victoria's beloved
friends. Though she was not at Eu during the visit, she
inspired part of Victoria's bubbling feeling of happiness at
belonging for a time to this huge rambling household: 'I felt
at home with them all', she wrote, 'as if I were one of them';
and again, 'I love them all so much, I feel so gay and happy
with these dear people.' But her steely side was to show itself.

The motive underlying the stay — the gay picnics, the
informal breakfasts, the uproarious theatricals — was to
obtain Louis Philippe's undertaking that his dynastic in-
trigues would cease, that he would not marry his son off to
the teenage Queen of Spain or her sister, in return for the
British promise that the young Queen would not marry a

*Clémentine, the daughter
of King Louis Philippe of
France, was married to
Augustus of Saxe-
Coburg-Gotha, cousin to
Victoria and Albert. On
12 May 1849 they came to
stay at Buckingham
Palace, with their
daughter Clotilde.
'Clotilde is a great
beauty', wrote the Queen.
She immediately painted
the two-year-old child and
commissioned a portrait
from Ross.*

Clotilde Coburg. VR del May 16
1849.

Coburg prince either. Louis Philippe gave his word. When he reneged in 1846, after a misunderstanding caused by an indiscretion of Lord Palmerston, the Foreign Secretary, Victoria hardened towards him. The mistrust inspired by the 'Spanish marriages' turned to hardly disguised contempt on his docile abdication and flight after the revolution of 1848. For although Victoria appreciated the bourgeois home life of the King, her ideas about a monarch's right to rule were less democratic.

The Orléans exiles, smuggled out of their hostile country in a series of Pimpernel-like adventures, were given shelter in England. Victoria shuddered to hear that the clothes of her dearest Vecto (Victoire) were being worn 'by the worst women', and was appalled at the financial straits of the whole family. But she was smug that the typhoon of 1848, which ravaged Continental Europe, hardly stirred the leaves in England.

On the eve of the huge Chartist demonstration on Kennington Common in April, the worst threat to British stability that year, she left London quietly for the safety of Osborne with her three-week-old daughter, Princess Louise. But the Chartists did not rouse the variety of support they needed and the meeting passed with a minimum of incident. The most severe trial undergone by Victoria and Albert during that turbulent year was the news — by anonymous letter — that prints of their etchings, the private record of their home life, had been surreptitiously made and were to be published and sold to the public. In one of the few cases ever brought by a member of the royal family as a private citizen against another, the Prince Consort took out an injunction against William Strange the publisher. When Strange appealed, in February 1849, the injunction was upheld, establishing a legal precedent that a work of art cannot be published without the artist's consent. *The Times* cooed complacently: 'We rejoice that Her Majesty and her husband should have stepped down from their altitude thus to defend their personal rights. . . . While other Sovereigns of Europe are fugitive or trembling on their thrones, the chief anxiety

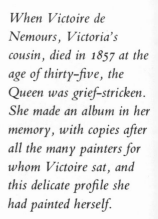

When Victoire de Nemours, Victoria's cousin, died in 1857 at the age of thirty-five, the Queen was grief-stricken. She made an album in her memory, with copies after all the many painters for whom Victoire sat, and this delicate profile she had painted herself.

of the Queen of England . . . is to protect herself against the annoyance . . . of having her drawings . . . published.'

Drawing served to remind: the Queen used her skill as a memory bank. This function of the pad and pencil was to some extent usurped by photography by the 1860s, but as the manageable amateur's camera had not yet been developed, sketching remained the prime method for travellers wishing to capture the sights for themselves. On all her trips Victoria took with her little albums made by firms still famous today for artists' materials, entitled 'Combination of Pocket Book Sketch Book and Palette . . . in the most convenient and portable form, particularly adapted for Tourists'. She had declared on her sixteenth birthday, 'I *love* to be *employed*: I *hate* to be *idle*', and whenever she was on board the *Victoria and Albert*, or riding in a carriage, or stopping for refreshments *en route*, she would busy herself drawing the scenery about her, or quickly noting down particulars of dress in the local people.

In 1844 Victoria drew the first Chinese boy she had ever seen. The policies of her reign towards the Celestial Empire were never as sensitive or observant of Chinese individuality as this fine sketch.

145

147

Napoleon III, Emperor of the French (left) and his wife the Spanish-born Eugénie de Montijo (right) made a vivid impression on the Queen, who first met them in April 1855 at Windsor, and later that year stayed with them in Paris. She drew them both after her visit, copying a medallion of the Emperor and Baron Humbert's bust of Eugénie.

Except for a brief visit in 1845, the Queen did not return to France for twelve years. When she did, it was to pay a state visit to Napoleon III in 1855, to cement the alliance of France and England against Russia in the Crimean War. Napoleon and Eugénie had visited Windsor in April that year (the Waterloo Room in the castle was speedily rechristened the 'Picture Gallery'). In August, Victoria and Albert returned the honour. Albert's birthday, 'the *dearest* of days', was spent in Paris, and Victoria gave him a set of studs with one button left blank: 'I hope for Sevastopol'. Victoria found the Emperor scarily compelling, Eugénie beautiful and well dressed, and the imperial style very rich indeed. She felt better when she had told Napoleon how much she felt for her friends the Orléans refugees and deplored the confiscation of all their goods. She was incredulous when he assured her they were dangerous enemies to him. 'The Emperor said . . . that their agents were in constant communication with his enemies, even "avec ceux qui prêchent l'assassinat." I said I could hardly credit this; they were incapable of any such act, I was sure.'

Previous page : This fine watercolour, showing how the Queen could sometimes use her linear assurance to greater advantage with subtle colour wash, was made aboard the Victoria and Albert *while she lay at anchor off Torquay. 'The situation is beautiful', wrote the Queen, and thought the port 'quite like a foreign town'.*

148

The Empress Eugenie
from a bust & from recollection
Rd.dl. May. 14. 1855.

The shiningly clean air of Paris made the Queen of smoky London wistful; she made several drawings of the bright gardens of St Cloud, and at Le Petit Trianon where she enjoyed the model mill and dairy of 'the poor unhappy Queen', Marie Antoinette. But the most powerful *frisson* came at a state ball given in the glittering Galerie des Glaces at Versailles, for the first time since the Ancien Régime, with fireworks, devised by the Empress, and including a tableau of Windsor, and décor modelled on a print of a *fête* given by Louis XV. There Victoria 'valsed very quietly' with Napoleon III and was yet again awed, as she had been at Windsor earlier in the spring, 'to think that I, the granddaughter of George III, should dance with the Emperor Napoleon, nephew to our great enemy, now my nearest and most intimate ally'.

Queen Victoria had written to Uncle Leopold at the height of the ferment in 1848: '*Great* events make me quiet and calm; it is only trifles that irritate my nerves.' This was true, and not entirely creditable. Similarly, she found greater

The palace of Saint-Cloud, where Victoria and Albert stayed in 1855, was 'like a fairy tale and everything so beautiful . . . the air so light and so very clear and sharp against the horizon. The absence of smoke helps to make everything white and bright', wrote Victoria on 20 August. This view of Paris was painted from her window.

On the same occasion, Victoria 'sat drawing on the balcony, and took a little sketch of the avenue looking towards the town of St-Cloud, all so pretty.' She had received a few lessons in perspective as a child from an English watercolourist, John Foulon, but this avenue of trees is a rare attempt at a painting with a vanishing point.

excitement in modest pleasures. Her imagination did not engage with the epic: she preferred the cameo. Her enjoyment of her next visit to France, a private and unofficial sailing trip to Normandy in August 1857, inspired paeans of praise. It was made at the height of the Indian mutiny, during the bitter siege of Lucknow. But not a mention of this shadows Victoria's gaiety. Her priorities were different. On her previous trip to France Vicky and Bertie had come with her, and she had received cables daily about the other children left behind. In 1857 the whole family, with the exception of the baby Leopold, embarked on the *Victoria and Albert*, and on arrival at Cherbourg boarded a rickety coach

for a day's outing to the village of Bricquebec, 22 kilometres along the coast. The Queen was in raptures at roughing it: 'It was the regular French Poste driven by one postillion on the wheel horse; the horses harnessed with ropes — no springs to the carriage, so that we bumped along the paved roads, pretty hard . . . The Postboys made such a noise, clacking and flourishing their whips . . .' When they went downhill 'a sort of drag had constantly to be let down on both sides to keep back the wheels . . . Intensely hot and dusty, but all, too

At the Normandy village of Bricquebec, which Victoria and the family visited incognito in August 1857, the Queen made these sketches of local costume, noting in particular the starched white caps of the women.

Charlotte of Belgium, daughter of Uncle Leopold and later the tragic Empress of Mexico, drawn by Victoria in her first beauty at the age of fifteen.

delightfully interesting . . . '

There was 'no end to the picturesque groups' that she and Vicky sketched, making the conventional nineteenth-century equivalence between the primitive and the pleasing. In the village itself, the mayor was 'tipsy'; the crowd eventually recognized the party, calling out, '*laquelle est donc la reine?*' They took refuge in a smoky upstairs room, and only managed to escape so late that dinner, in that most regular of households, took place 'at a quarter to ten!'

Left: The Queen was quick at capturing a likeness: this frankly admiring study is of Robert Brison, a sailor on the royal yacht.

Below: This serene and glowing treatment of an English headland at twilight is one of Victoria's most richly coloured and finished watercolours.

The following year, the *Victoria and Albert* made the channel crossing again. Twelve ships escorted them, nine ships of the line received them, and the House of Commons chartered a boat for a hundred of its members. The full royal salute thundered in Cherbourg harbour 'repeated I think five times — really magnificent . . . ' while scores of small craft, bright pennants fluttering, welcomed the English Queen. Napoleon sailed over to greet them in a burnished barge, and seventy people sat down to dinner on deck. But Victoria noticed that Napoleon was not in good spirits 'and seems sensitive about all that has been said of him in England and elsewhere'.

The next day, the Queen and the Prince returned to Osborne, found all their children waiting at the door, and in honour of Alfred's birthday joined in a country dance on the terrace. As the shadows lengthened in the summer evening, their weaving figures amid the parterres and the statuary of Osborne danced for Alfred's birthday; but they celebrate for

us now the untroubled certainties of Victoria's rule. She had been introduced to Count Bismarck at the Versailles ball in 1855; only twelve years after her last meeting with Napoleon and Eugénie at Cherbourg, Bismarck's Prussian might destroyed the Second Empire, and the Imperial family, following the Orléans, took refuge in England. Hearing of the siege of Paris, the unimpeachable Victoria exclaimed to Gladstone: 'It is a great *moral*!' Her throne, it seemed, was set fast in granite.

The day trip to Bricquebec had been 'altogether charming' except that it was 'poor dear Vicky's last one with us, which is very sad.' Although childhood had been consecrated as inviolable, adolescence had not yet received its twentieth-century status, and the Princess Royal, at the age of fourteen, was engaged to Prince Frederick William of Prussia, 'Fritz'. The marriage had been planned by both sides when the couple were babies; it had been formally broached by Fritz and consented to in 1855, though then, as Victoria wrote to Leopold, 'the child herself is to know nothing'. On a visit to Windsor the following year, Fritz wooed Vicky and to the satisfaction of everyone the sixteen-year-old Princess and the young Prince fell in love. 'Every spare moment Vicky has (and *I* have, for I must chaperon this loving couple . . .) is devoted to her bridegroom, who is *so* much in love, that even if he is out driving and walking with her, he is not satisfied, and says he has not seen her . . . '

Vicky and Fritz were married on 25 January 1858 with 'amazing éclat', wrote Greville, in the Chapel Royal St James's — her mother had huffed indignantly at the suggestion that the wedding should take place in Prussia. It was 'the second most eventful day of my life as regards feeling. I felt as if I were being married over again myself . . . ' The parting afterwards was terrible, for both parents and child. 'I am not of a demonstrative nature', wrote Albert to his adored daughter, 'and therefore you can hardly know how dear you have always been to me and what a void you have left . . . ' 'I thought my heart was going to break . . . I miss you so dreadfully my dear Papa, more than I can say',

's favourite costume as Queen.

Ada, the Queen's niece, fifth child of her beloved sister Feodore, was one of Victoria's favourite subjects, and drawings of her were transferred on to engraving plates.

she answered. Then began the feverish, impassioned correspondence of mother and daughter that was to go back and forth between Germany and England for the next forty-two years — over 7000 letters altogether.

However painful this early fledging, it realized a long and potent dream of Albert and his Queen: to ally Germany with England by a dynastic marriage, and through the Princess Royal, acolyte in Albert's school of political theory, to educate Prussia in the constitutional and liberal forms of government and divert it from the 'blood and iron' imperialism advocated by Bismarck and later the Junkers of the Kreuzzeitung party. Vicky would become Empress, and her children the future rulers of a progressive Germany in the English mould.

Seven months after the wedding, Victoria and Albert visited their 'beloved Child'. The Prussians exacted a meeting on their home ground. Coburg or the Rhine, where the Queen wanted to meet her daughter, were turned down as unsuitable, and so Victoria was forced to make the long journey to Potsdam and Berlin, site of innumerable Prussian palaces. She sailed on the *Victoria and Albert* up the Scheld from Gravesend, and then took the train from Antwerp via Dusseldorf and Cologne. At each stage of the fatiguing route, the Queen was met by elaborate ceremonial and royal relations. It was 'blazingly hot, and there was such a haze'. The heatwave persisted, and Victoria, who thrived on draughts and frost, suffered from 'racking' headaches and bouts of short-temperedness. At the same time, they heard that Albert's valet Cart, who had come with him from Coburg in 1840 and along with his greyhound Eos had been Albert's only links with his youth, had died; the royal couple's spirits were very low.

Victoria cheered up at the illuminations in Dusseldorf, where she was received by Prince Hohenzollern. The 'transparent paper lamps, and some like baskets of flowers, also splendid red and blue lights . . . All was the spontaneous act of the Artists and the inhabitants'. And they both rallied when Fritz boarded the train and rode with them to the

157

V.[?] del from [?]collection – 1858..

Vicky at her Marriage.
Chapel Royal Jan.[?] 25: 1858—

Wildpark station at Brandenburg, where Vicky — 'our darling child, with a nosegay in her hand' — awaited them. At Babelsberg, a summer palace built above water in the countryside near Potsdam, Vicky and her mother talked and kissed each other goodnight, and it was 'very pleasant' and the Queen felt 'as if she were my own again . . .'

But the round of functions and sightseeing, one imposing palace after another, was arduous. Victoria made dutiful notes on the possessions and décor of each princely seat; in view of the later destruction of so many of them, it is a shame how imprecise her jottings are. She was most affected by the mourning customs of Prussia: the chair in which Frederick the Great had died, still stained with his blood, and the 'unfinished work' of the last Queen, preserved untouched in her apartments in the Palace of Charlottenburg, Berlin. She,

On 25 January 1858, in the Chapel Royal, St James's, the Princess Royal married Prince Frederick William of Prussia. This watercolour made by her mother from memory, shows Vicky in a dress of white moiré antique, with three tiers and a veil of Honiton lace, caught up and wreathed with myrtle and orange blossom.

who was to emulate this reverence so morbidly herself, found it 'melancholy'. Always with a keen eye for military turn-out — in Paris she had remarked the superior tailoring of the men's uniforms — Victoria observed how everyone in Germany seemed to be in uniform all day long, and that Prussian drill excelled English, 'though the men only serve three years'. Prophetically, she recoiled from the goose-step: at a parade of 4000 troops in Potsdam, she watched as they 'marched past in very quick time, with that peculiar step, throwing the leg out and stamping . . . '

Only in the shade of the beautiful gardens at Babelsberg and Charlottenburg, and in the evening boat rides and picnics at the Neue Palais, did the Queen escape from the unrelenting heat and the political tensions of the Prussian court. She sat out and drew with Vicky watercolour pictures of the temples and follies and lakes, blotting from her mind the dangerousness of her daughter's position. For Vicky, a foreign Princess still fiercely loyal to the country she thought of — and more tactlessly spoke of — as 'home', was surrounded by a faction-ridden court. King Frederick William IV had had a stroke and become senile, and the Regent, his brother Prince William, Fritz's father, was anticonstitutional, Bismarckian and pro-Russian. Vicky had few

All around Potsdam, Frederick the Great and his successors had built themselves summer palaces which Victoria visited in the summer of 1858, making these attractive watercolour studies of the Marmorpalais and the bridge at Klein-Glienicke, another beautifully laid out park, painted as the light changed between afternoon and sunset.

friends. Even the choice of an English nurse made her the object of suspicion from the surrounding Germans. Neither Victoria nor Albert wished to see this; they dreamt of subduing Prussian despotism in a united German empire.

Their hopes centred on Fritz, who would succeed his father, and on the child whom Vicky was expecting in that summer of 1858. In fact, Fritz survived his father only a few months when he died in 1888, and the child Vicky bore was to take the imperialist road of his grandfather and, as the Kaiser, to cut the fragile thread bound by Victoria and Albert

about the two great powers of Europe. But in 1858 none of this disturbed them. Victoria minded above all else that she could not stay with Vicky for the birth: 'I feel it bitterly that I have to forgo my natural right and duty to be with my dear Child in her hour of trial, as every other mother does.' She hoped to be able to attend the christening, but in the end only managed to see her first grandchild in the autumn of 1860, when she returned to Germany for a much more pleasant three-week stay in Albert's ancestral home at Coburg, where Vicky and Fritz and 'little William' awaited them.

When 'little William', Vicky's first child, was born the 'children were in extacies', wrote the Queen, 'at Uncle and Aunt-ship, Arthur shouting out: "I'M an uncle".'

The future Kaiser's military bearing already shows in the Queen's pencil drawing of him (right), but she also caught his childlike sweetness in the exquisite sketch of him (left), in the arms of her youngest child, Beatrice, only two years older than her nephew.

The countryside around the Rosenau, Albert's birthplace, became so familiar to Victoria on their two happy and leisurely visits that she was able to plan her compositions with forethought, as in this romantic view of the gabled Gothic schloss.

Victoria had first visited Coburg in the summer of 1845, when she was flush with love for Albert, and every tree in whose shade he had strolled, every building he had lived in or known, every detail of the modest yet beautifully furnished rooms of the castle of Rosenau, every item in the museum of specimens that he and Ernest had collected, had been a source of intensified passion for her husband. Since then Albert's realization that his wife's grasp of affairs, though quick, was so much more frivolous and superficial than his own had led him to take on more and more work, until the Queen became jealous of it — not because Albert usurped her role, but because she did not have him to herself. Her passionate nature erupted in tantrums, met by meticulously argued and patient letters in reply from Albert, to whom in real life *sturm und drang* was torment. On top of this he was a sick man, suffering from rheumatism in the shoulder which prevented him shooting, from stomach pains, and from frequent undiagnosed disturbances which enfeebled him and which Victoria's iron health and intolerance of weakness only exacerbated.

Victoria was happy to be back in Coburg, to be out tranquilly with Vicky, with their sketchbooks and their new-

Market day in Coburg fascinated her, and she made many studies of the people, their distinctive costumes and the scene, including this ambitiously constructed and fully realised view of the stalls set up in the square beneath her sitting room window in the Ehrenburg Palace.

163

found bond of motherhood, but Albert's presence does not cast the peachy glow over her diary that it had in 1845. Nevertheless they were in a holiday mood until, in the third week of their visit, the horses drawing the Prince's open carriage bolted at a level crossing. The bar was down, a waggon stood in the way. Albert threw himself to the ground; the carriage crashed through, the coachman was badly injured and one horse killed. Albert escaped with bad bruising, but he was a man under strain, and the accident drained his resources. Only Baron Stockmar, ever the percipient observer, saw the whole gravity of the case: 'God have mercy on us!' he wrote. 'If anything serious should ever happen to him, he will die.' Albert, visited by his brother, broke down. In tears he told him that he knew he would never see Coburg again.

For the first time since 1835 Victoria fell very ill herself; but though her body may have been warning her of the seriousness of the Prince's condition, her mind, always determined to outface disaster, firmly pushed it aside. On their return to England Albert had resumed his self-imposed punishing routine, snatching moments between matters political, domestic and artistic to play duets with Victoria and read aloud to her the 'last new book' of George Eliot, *Silas Marner*.

In August 1861, they travelled together for the last time, to Ireland. It was the Queen's second visit: in 1849 she was the first British monarch ever to set foot in Cork, and though guarded in her political comments, had been pleased at the people's 'enthusiasm' and very struck by their handsomeness — 'almost every third woman is pretty, and some remarkably so'. In 1861, Victoria took Alfred, Alice and Lenchen with her, and her main purpose was to see Bertie, the Prince of Wales, who was with the Guards at their camp in Curragh; Albert also hoped that the beautiful surroundings of Killarney would coax his wife out of her rage and grief at the death of her mother that March. But Victoria was never more obstinate than in her attachment to mourning. 'I *derive* benefit and *relief* both to my body and soul in *dwelling*

In the last month's of his life, Albert was utterly crushed by the news that his Portuguese cousins, King Pedro V and two of his brothers, had all been carried off by typhoid. Louis, the last remaining brother, succeeded to the throne of Portugal, and reigned until 1889.

on the sad object which is *the* one which fills my heart!' she wrote, on the death of her half-brother Charles in 1856. So Albert's increasing debilitation passed unobserved by his wife, except that in a tone of sympathy that scarcely conceals her frustration, she records continually that dearest Albert was 'fagged'.

On 25 November, with that attention to hopeful details that accompanies all efforts to placate implacable furies, Victoria began to record the onslaught of his final illness. He was sleepless, restless, in pain, unable to eat and hardly to drink; the ignorance of his medical staff and the heroic optimism of his family prevented him being nursed or rested with any proper care. He could hardly smile, though he managed to enjoy Baby reciting some French verse for her lessons. He often greeted his wife with a blind, strange look that scared her. On 8 December he asked to hear music, and Princess Alice played his favourites chorales on the piano next door; on 13 December the Queen's diary ends with the sentence that had appeared again and again, that the doctors 'said there was no reason to anticipate anything worse'. There were no more entries after that. Albert died the next day, perhaps of typhoid, perhaps of a long cancer, but most certainly of overwork.

Albert had always struggled to make Victoria, to whom he had devoted his life, understand the ugliness of excess; like so many of the lessons he had repeated with such thought and justification it was a waste of time, and never more so than after his death. 'My *life* as a *happy* one is *ended*!' she wrote; 'the world is gone for *me*! . . . Oh! to be cut off in the prime of life — to see our pure, happy, quiet, domestic life, which *alone* enabled me to bear my *much* disliked position, *cut off* at forty-two . . . is *too awful*, too cruel!'

SIX

The Highland Haven

Prince Albert's memory was not well served by his widow's cult. The spires, institutions, plinths and platforms that bore his statue or his name pressed his perfections too hard on a nation that is suspicious of paragons, preferring Falstaff in his cups to Thomas More or adulterous Lancelot to pure Percival. It infuriated the Queen that Albert should not be loved while the Prince of Wales, indolent, pleasure-loving, ignorant and even immoral, should win effortlessly the popularity that had eluded her beloved husband. Throughout her long widowhood — she lived almost exactly twice as long as Albert — and especially during its first two decades she drove herself to lead her life as a living memorial to his values and his teaching. 'I am (also) anxious to repeat one thing, and *that one* is my firm resolve, my *irrevocable decision*, viz. that *his* wishes — *his* plans — about everything, *his* views about *every* thing are to me *my law*! . . . ' Like many a disciple before her, the Queen chose to interpret her master's law according to her own lights.

She was broken by his death, through sincere love and remorse at her shortcomings — the tantrums, the nagging, the intolerance of weakness with which she had plagued him — and through sheer helplessness, for together they had contrived to make her exaggeratedly dependent on him. She retreated, and squirrel-like hid herself away during the winter of her bereavement in the place where Albert had been happiest, 'my dear Albert's *own* creation, own work,

In this varied landscape of the Dee from Balmoral, Victoria used the conventional technique of pure wash over pencil to great effect and achieved a rich and varied texture of colour, heightened by the touches of white in the water.

The clump of Highland heather is one of the Queen's rare flower studies.

167

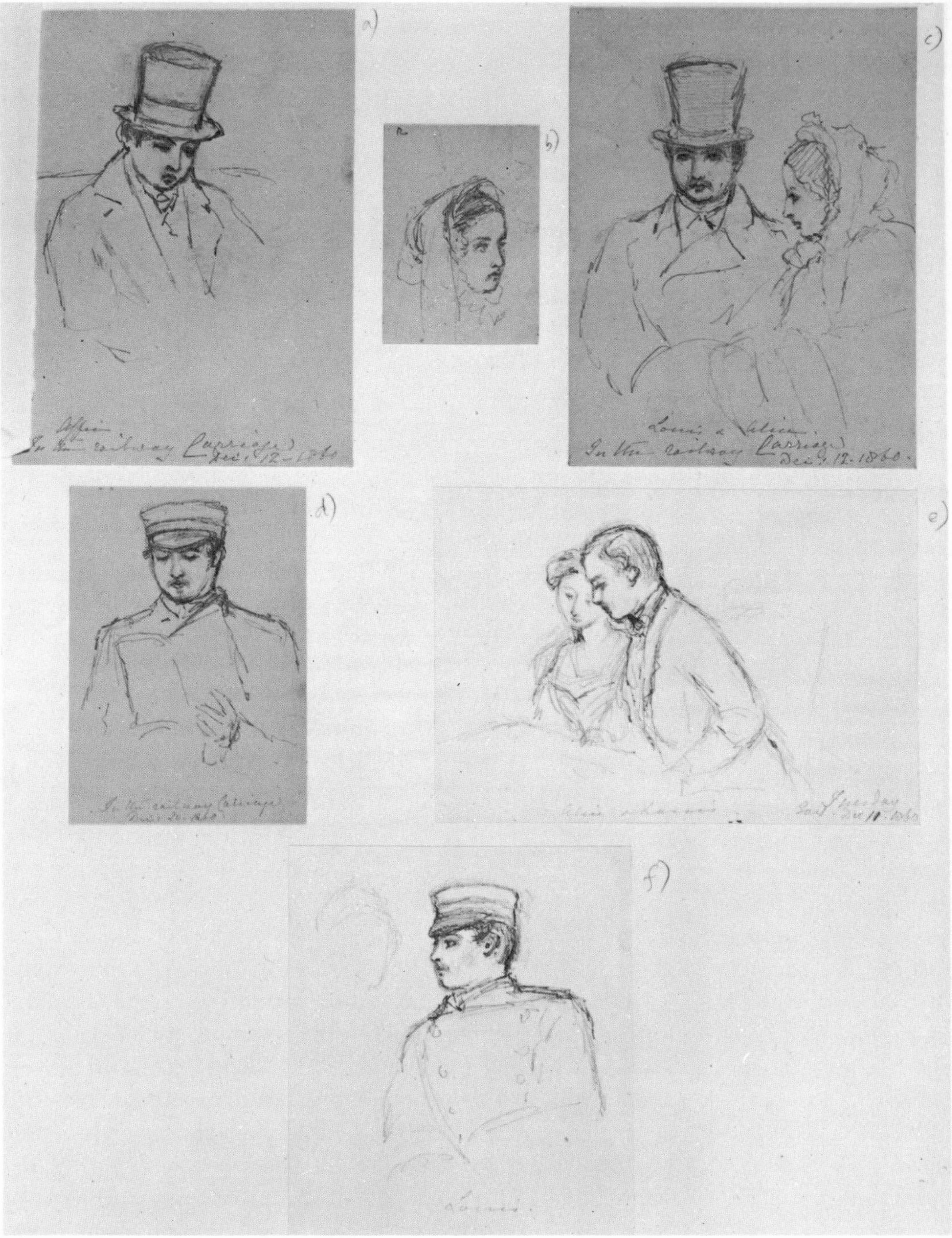
a)
b)
c)
d)
e)
f)
Louis

Left: This sheet of pencil studies of Princess Alice with her fiancé Louis of Hesse and her brother Alfred was made on a train journey, where Victoria always liked to sketch, and it shows at its best her gift for spontaneous, direct portraiture.

own building, own laying out' — Balmoral Castle in the Highlands.

In 1842, during her post-natal exhaustion after Vicky and Bertie's births, the Queen had made her first journey to Scotland, sailing up to the West Coast on the recommendation of her doctor. She and the Prince stayed in Lord Breadalbane's castle at Taymouth; two years later, Lord and Lady Glenlyon lent them Blair Atholl. Victoria's artistic eye was captivated. 'Every turn you have a picture', she wrote. She agreed with Albert that 'the chief beauty of mountain scenery consisted in its frequent changes', and she began to chronicle the effects of weather and season and light on the glens and lochs that unfolded themselves before her entranced vision as Albert drove her, often for more than two hours at a stretch, along the Highland roads.

One of the Queen's ladies-in-waiting during this visit was Charlotte Canning, later Vicereine of India, and together they sat down on the hillside, on plaids spread out for them, to sketch and paint. Lady Canning was one of the celebrated Stuart daughters — her sister was the remarkable beauty and gifted artist Lady Waterford — and she too had a developed artistic gift. One of the reasons for the paucity of watercolours painted by Victoria on her first visit to Coburg may be that Charlotte Canning accompanied her and made some very graceful, finished and keen-eyed paintings of the sights, which the Queen later kept in her souvenir albums. But in Scotland Victoria was not cramped by Lady Canning's skills. In 1844, and again in 1847 when she and Albert stayed at Lord

Below: At the beginning of the sketchbooks kept by the Queen during her retreat into the Highlands after Albert's death, she recorded the passing years of her bereavement.

1862

1st year of my misery.

Abercorn's shooting lodge of Ardverickie, she was painting with a fresh, bold use of colour, her powers of observation sharpened by the magnificent views and the tonic romance of scenery far wilder and grander than anything she had seen hitherto. After a ride in the hills, she surpassed herself in sensuous description: 'As the sun went down the scenery became more and more beautiful, the sky crimson, golden-red and blue, and the hills becoming purple and lilac, most exquisite, till at length it set, and the hues grew softer in the sky and the outlines of the hills sharper. I never saw anything so fine.'

Victoria's growing skills were also the result of excellent tuition. In July 1846 Edward Lear, whose *Excursions in Italy* had just been published, came to Osborne and coached the Queen in draughtsmanship. She was also receiving regular lessons from William Leighton Leitch. 'Good old Leitch' as

These two studies of the same view from Victoria's window at Balmoral, on successive days in September and October 1848, show how conscientiously Victoria applied herself to capturing the beauty she and Albert found in the Highland scenery. The first, showing rain clouds blurring the outline of the mountains, has great attack and softness.

In this brighter second attempt, her effort made on a rougher cartridge paper is more self-consciously artistic, and less fresh.

the Queen called him was a marvellously sensitive draughtsman and a glowing painter who exploited to the full the breadth of a watercolour palette, from sombre tones in the depths of foliage to a hard brilliance for flowers and sunlight. Leitch was introduced to Court by Lady Canning, having been recommended by the Duchess of Sutherland, Victoria's great friend and her Mistress of the Robes. Her cousin, Richard Cavendish, had been instructed by Leitch during his travels in Italy. Leitch gave the Queen a basic technical knowledge of the potential of watercolour that Westall had failed to do: 'I showed how light, that is, brilliancy, was produced by yellow ochre, pink madder, and cobalt blue, and darkness, deeper than black, by sepia, purple lake, and indigo — also primitive colours. Using these two classes of colours with their compounds, I then did skies, distance, middle-ground, foreground, white clouds, and their shadows, no whiter than a lady's satin dress; and then with the same colours, a black dress full of colour and shadow, but with no *black* in it; and then a great many varieties of green colours. After attending to this part of the lesson with great earnestness . . . the Queen turned to Lady Canning and said, "This is very wonderful . . ."'

Leitch was a native of Glasgow, and after scraping a living in Scotland as a scene-painter and snuff box decorator, he came south to improve his fortunes. He became a favourite instructor in aristocratic circles; he was a good raconteur and an entertaining mimic, and he soon found that he had a 'great relish for society'. One of his pupils, Sir Coutts Lindsay, later the owner of the Grosvenor Gallery, thought 'he was often held away from the more ardent pursuit of his art by the insistence of those who would by no means allow themselves to be deprived of his teaching and his gaiety'. Leitch attended Victoria over a period of twenty-two years, accompanying her to Osborne and Windsor as well as Balmoral, until the excruciating migraines from which he suffered forced him to give up teaching.

On Victoria and Albert's first visit to Scotland they sailed up the West Coast, past such striking landmarks as Dunollie Castle, guarding the mouth of the Sound of Kerrera.

My. copied from Landseer's Drawing on the Drawingroom at Ardverick — Sept 5th 1847.

At Ardverickie, Victoria admired particularly the walls
'ornamented with beautiful drawings of stags by Landseer'.
Landseer was so inspired by the scenery and the life of the
Highlands that it is sometimes difficult to remember he was
not Scots by birth. He was at his best when working
spontaneously and prevented from reworking and over-
painting, and the frescoes at Ardverickie, drawn straight on
to the wet wall with a burnt stick and red brick, were
probably amongst the most vivid and fresh examples of his
work. But they were destroyed by fire in 1873, and Victoria's
copies, together with a single photograph taken by a
workman at the lodge, remain the only record of them. Like
Leitch, Landseer took to high company with relish. He too
taught the Queen on her Highland visits, adding highlights
and touches of definition to her many drawings of stags 'dear
Albert shot', and helping her to draw in pastel.

173

'There was a quiet, a retirement, a wildness, a liberty and a solitude', wrote Queen Victoria, who felt as intensely about the Highlands as Wordsworth about the Lakes, identifying

> *Not with the mean and vulgar works of man,*
> *But with high objects, with enduring things,*
> *With life and nature . . .*

Victoria and Albert were determined to return, and not only for the 'beautiful scenery', but for the Scots themselves: 'such a chivalrous, fine, active people'. By extraordinary fortune a miser and eccentric, John Camden Nield, died in 1852 and left the Queen half a million pounds. Not long after this, she and Albert first leased, and then bought, the estate of Balmoral on Deeside near Aberdeen, where the weather was more clement than on the rugged and rain-swept West Coast.

Right: Albert built at Balmoral a model farm and dairy on the lines he had already begun at Windsor, and Victoria made these delicate sketches of cattle there.

Below: This spirited evocation of one of the Queen's favourite haunts below Balloch Buie was spread over two pages in one of her small travelling sketchbooks.

Once again the old house was thrown down, and a new one raised in its place. Albert was again the architect, collaborating with William Smith, the City Architect of Aberdeen. The conception sprang even more directly from his imagination than Osborne had: the Dee's pretty run at the foot of the castle's site became visible from the windows, and the white granite walls, the crow-stepped gables, pepperpot turrets, finials and castellated parapets recalled the silhouettes of the Rosenau and the Ehrenburg Palace of Coburg. The foundation stone was laid by the Queen on 28 September 1853, with much dancing of reels and even sips of whisky at the gillies' ball that evening.

Following Albert's example, Victoria threw herself with unconditional enthusiasm into the life of the Highlands, and thus hallowed the Scottish mystique that Sir Walter Scott's writings had recently brought before English eyes. The

This painting by Victoria of the new Balmoral, designed by Albert to resemble his native German castles, was made in 1854 while it was being built.

Alfred & Bertie. —

autumn round of deer-stalking, rambles, hikes, climbs and
picnics in scenic spots was carried out with vigour and
maximum authenticity. Haggis was sampled. A Balmoral
tartan was designed, and added to those already decorating
the antlered halls of the castle. Prince Albert, the Prince of
Wales and all the royal children set the fashion for kilts that
has proved one of the most durable of all, in children's dress
in particular. Silk tartans were made up into dresses for the
Princesses, and the Queen's adoption of the plaid spread its
wearing throughout English society.

The first novel Victoria had ever read was Scott's *Bride of
Lammermoor*; for the rest of her life she recorded her delight in
the picturesque people of Scotland and their customs, in the
sword dances by torchlight and the bagpipes — a piper or

The Shee? of Allt na Guithasn in
Loch Muick.

B. del. Aug. 31. 1849.

two always accompanied their excursions. She took down carefully the place names, revelling in the strange, tongue-twisting sounds: the Pass of Killiecrankie, the Shiel of Alt-na-Giuthasach, the mountains of Loch-na-Gar and Ben Muich Dhui; she tried to pick up a word or two of Gaelic, and admired Albert's quicker tongue. She followed patiently on ponies, or on foot — it is remarkable how much scrambling she did, crinolines regardless, on Scottish hillsides — as Albert fished for salmon, or manfully stalked the valleys. The Prince Consort's sportsmanship was derided; he was reputed — and still is in Scotland — a very bad shot, and reports that his gillies and keepers constantly covered up for him filled the pages of *Punch* with gleeful and very xenophobic ribaldry. On their visit to Coburg in 1845 a *battue* had been organized for the Queen's entertainment: the animals were driven into a ring where they could be picked off by the huntsmen from a pavilion — a practice considered by the English un-sportsmanlike and ungentlemanly. Albert never really re-covered from the huge unpopularity the *battue* caused him. But Victoria remained aloof, perhaps even deaf, to the taunts. She referred constantly and tactlessly to the Prince's home-sickness, writing how he loved the Scottish landscape because it reminded him of Thuringia, and how he said that 'many of the people look like Germans'. She was thrilled when, after a good day's sport for Albert, the huntsmen told her she had 'a lucky foot', and with wifely devotion noted over two pages of a sketchbook the exact weights of six deer 'killed with 6 shots, out stalking in the Muichle Pass'.

Together they pursued the simple life. To escape Balmoral's middle-class comforts they built austere shiels in picturesque spots at Alt-na-Giuthasach and Glen Gelder, where they could stay, virtually unattended in a few humble rooms, like the crofters who were their tenants. Together they explored the countryside, enjoying the thrills of being incognito. After a picnic lunch 'on a very precipitous place' above Glen Isla, Albert scribbled on a bit of paper that he had lunched 'at this spot'. He then stuck the note in the ground, 'in a seltzer water bottle' for the wonder of later travellers.

Victoria was inspired to experiment with different media and in the fifties briefly took up oils: she painted her children performing *Athalie*, and set their interpretation of *Das Hahnenschlag* in a realistic rather than theatrical bucolic setting. She also painted portraits of Annie and Archie MacDonald, which she later hung in her bathroom at Osborne. They were the children of Albert's gillie from the west of Scotland, 'a remarkably tall and handsome' man, in the Queen's opinion. Archie became *Jäger* to the Prince of Wales; Annie died of tuberculosis in 1866.

Landseer tutored the Queen's efforts in oil, and introduced her to pastel, a medium he favoured. In 1851 and 1852 the Queen made dozens of bold, garishly coloured portraits of retainers and tenants and neighbours at Balmoral — the Grants and the Flemmings and Jane MacKenzie at her tub,

Archie and Annie MacDonald, painted here in the model kennels at Balmoral, were the children of Archibald MacDonald, the Prince Consort's gillie, and his wife Anne.

Maggie Gow

Mag... del Sept: 14. 1849.
Balmoral

Maggie Gow, daughter of the Balmoral tenant James Gow, was one of the many 'Highland lassies' whom the Queen visited regularly and painted.

and other 'Highland lads and lassies' whose simplicity and goodness of heart touched her so deeply. She dispensed warm socks and red pinafores when she went visiting, but was the first to admit that her attempts at portraiture were not altogether a success: Landseer had shown her 'how to draw in chalks', she wrote, 'but I never could manage that well.'

The faithful Scottishness of Victoria and Albert's style was painted by Landseer, and also by Carl Haag, a Bavarian specialist in sporting and mountain scenes who came to England via Brussels and commemorated in the fifties the strenuous riding excursions and shooting exploits of Albert and the Queen. In their embrace of the Scottish cult, Victoria and her husband embody the contemporary spirit of their times. Wordsworth and Coleridge and Keats had raised them, however indirectly, to know that nature in her wild state is the great teacher and the supreme uplifting mystery, while Scotland and its customs represented an ancient culture that was independent of classicism; its rediscovery constituted a romantic rejection of Greek and Roman formalism in favour of a distinguished barbarism — poetic, primitive, simple and autonomous. Victoria and Albert's eager identification with it, which seems to us now comical and rather absurd in two 'foreigners', reflects the lively confidence of their age in all things British and homegrown. In their lifetime its antiquarian side was not fustian, but energetically modern.

Prince Albert's interest in the Highlands reflected his progressive innovatory character as surely as his inspired organization of the Great Exhibition in 1851, and Victoria returned there after his death to recreate, as a living testimonial to his superior judgement in all things, the life they had led together. At the peak of her seclusion, in 1868, when murmurings against her prolonged withdrawal from public life were becoming louder, she published *Leaves from*

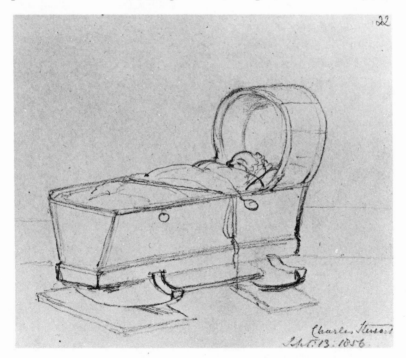

Victoria often visited the workers on the Balmoral estate; this baby asleep in a wooden cradle is the newborn son of Donald Stewart, one of the keepers.

184

the Journal of Our Life in the Highlands, extracts from her diary, with illustrations of her life in Scotland with the Prince and the happy excursions they had made together. Her children and some members of her household disliked its publication. The book gave the impression that the Queen's life was all play and no work, and during her long absences from England, either in Scotland or on the Isle of Wight, such an impression seemed inadvisable.

William Gladstone, Prime Minister during much of the period of Victoria's determined retreat, was compassionate and understanding, and travelled to Balmoral frequently to despatch state business. In 1869, after much pressure gently but firmly applied, he prevailed upon the Queen to show herself again in her capital and open Blackfriars Bridge and Holborn Viaduct, both high examples of the Age of Iron. In 1871, the Prince of Wales had been very ill indeed with typhoid, and a national day of thanksgiving for his delivery was proclaimed. Victoria, in spite of her disclaimers that life, especially as a Queen, held any pleasure for her, found that she thoroughly enjoyed herself: ' . . . a day of triùmph', she wrote to Vicky. 'Really most marvellous! Such touching affection and loyalty cannot be seen anywhere I think . . . Millions must have been out and the decorations were really beautiful — the cheering deafening . . . when we were stopping at Temple Bar amid deafening cheers I took dear Bertie's hand and pressed it — people cried.'

On that occasion, John Brown 'in his very fullest and very handsome full dress' rode on the box, and it was in some good part his achievement that the Queen felt strong enough to return to public life. Her first volume of *Leaves* was dedicated to the memory of Albert, her second, *More Leaves*, published in 1884, to that of John Brown. Her nature demanded support from someone whom she had created in her mind's eye as a source of strength, wisdom and truth, serving her as exclusive priestess. Although it annoyed her that others did not share her view of Albert's or Brown's perfections, she certainly thrived on her undivided possession of them.

Left: From the small
albums Victoria kept
when she was in
Scotland, she chose her
most successful attempts
and pasted them in to
beautifully bound books
on large pages (left).

Her range of colour had
become more sophisticated
since her earliest days: she
took the bluest of the blues
to capture the eyes of John
Brown (above) at the age
of 23.

But it would be wrong to equate Albert and Brown in any
other respect. She admired 'Johnnie Brown' because Albert
had; as a young man he had been picked by the Prince
Consort to be the Queen's servant, to lead her horse, to wade
through streams holding her above the water wrapped in a
plaid, to sit on the box of her carriage and oversee the
coachman. He was a magnificent specimen of the Highlander
so venerated by Albert: 'marked by that honesty and
sympathy, which always distinguish the inhabitants of
mountainous countries . . . . ' His blond good looks and blue
blue eyes, his 'vigorous, light, elastic tread' which the Queen
found 'quite astonishing', added to the picture of Celtic
purity in an era before Nazi ideology had made such attitudes
suspect. He was courageous and quick, and above all 'handy'
— high praise in Victoria's lexicon. He twice saved the

Queen from nasty coach accidents by his presence of mind, and when she was threatened by a pistol-brandishing Fenian in 1872, it was Brown 'alone' who noticed the danger and seized the assailant 'by the throat'. In 1865 she appointed him to the special post of 'The Queen's Highland Servant', 'to attend me *always* and everywhere out of doors, . . . and it is a *real* comfort, for he is *so* devoted to me — so simple, so intelligent, so *unlike* an *ordinary* servant, and so cheerful and attentive . . . ' Queen Victoria had a special feeling for her servants' friendship. She warned Vicky against changing hers often, for then 'there can be no mutual attachment . . . But I think you don't care much for the inestimable comfort and value of a truly devoted and attached and trustworthy servant.'

Initial enthusiasm in Court circles for John Brown's reviving influence on the widowed Queen soon waned: the informality of his manners, so relished by Victoria, seemed insolent to many around her; his drunkenness, his privileges, his prejudices and his unspoken but very real prerogatives infuriated almost everyone — the Prince of Wales in particular — and gave rise to angry and malicious comment in the press. But in spite of his attaining the rank of Esquire when the Queen moved him to serve her indoors as well as

In spite of her assiduous widowhood Queen Victoria never lost her sense of fun, as is shown by this lively picture of her taking 'tea in a snow storm' up in the Cairngorms.

J. Coutts & C. Campbell watching the deer. [B]o. Oct. 11. 1867.

The Queen welcomed Albert's passion for deerstalking, and often followed the hunting party on horseback or on foot, recording in her sketchbook such scenes as these two keepers tensely watching for game.

out, and gaining considerable increases in revenue, he remained a servant. On his death he was commemorated by an astonishing tribute: 'the faithful and devoted personal attendant and friend' is immortalized in copperplate engraving at the base of a column in the personal pantheon of Victoria, the mausoleum at Frogmore.

Benjamin Disraeli, who became Prime Minister for most of 1868 and again from 1874 to 1880, fascinated and flattered the Queen into renewed interest in her ever more splendid realm. Both he and John Brown, at the same period of the Queen's life, knew how to handle her, how to reassure and complete her when she was stalked by Albert's ghost, which made her feel bereft and hesitant and inadequate. John Brown called her 'wumman' and Disraeli 'the Faery'; John Brown told her it was 'very pleasant to walk with a person who is always content'; Disraeli in conversation would say 'we authors, ma'am'. Her zest, her wit, her liveliness returned in the decade of the seventies. 'She was wreathed in smiles', wrote Disraeli after one of their many long audiences, 'and, as she tattled, she glided about the room like a bird.' She did not paint Dizzy's seamed, compelling, bony and ironic face, but among her sketches made at this date appears one watercolour of a primrose. Victoria never painted flowers, except as flashes of colour in a landscape. But she sent by train to Disraeli in London nosegays of flowers she had picked herself at Osborne. His favourites, he told her, were the primroses, 'the ambassadors of Spring . . . the gems and jewels of Nature'. His gallantry knew no bounds: 'They show', he wrote, 'that your Majesty's sceptre has touched the enchanted isle'.

Victoria chose a primrose, rather than the man. After Albert died, people recede from the pages of her sketchbooks. The two folio albums, bound in soft suede with blue spine and corners, into which she stuck the best work from her smaller sketchpads after his death, begin with a watercolour view of the mausoleum at Frogmore where the Prince lay buried and where she was to join him. She painted it from her window at Windsor Castle, and it sounds the quiet, melancholy note of the sequence that follows. There is view after view of the places they enjoyed together — Glen

Nosegays were part of the important Victorian ritual of celebrating a birthday or a feeling, and this bunch of primroses is perhaps a tribute to Disraeli, whose favourite flowers they were.

The different techniques used by Victoria are clearly shown on this first page of her album of views (right) after the Prince Consort's death.

With considerable skill, the Queen used the background of the untouched white paper to create the impression of the snow-covered slopes outside the castle (below).

Albert's sportsmanship was mocked in the pages of Punch *and in posterity's memory, but the Queen was always loyal. In this rare still life study she pays her respects to a British army rifle with an exploded barrel which probably belonged to Albert.*

Muich, Balloch Buie, Craig Gowan — but they rarely feature the active figures stalking and shooting and fishing, the healthy Highlanders and local friends who appear in the earlier drawings. The landscape itself has been widowed. The watercolours are not in themselves melancholy, but their emptiness contrasts bleakly with her previous vitality. She continues to observe with a keen eye, but that eye is turned on the changing colours of the heather, the profiles of the mountains, and the tones and movements in the sky. A true inheritor of romanticism, she found in the Highland land-scape, uncultivated, wild, majestic, almost untouched by man's influence, an uplifting and tranquil solace in her long bereavement.

In 1862 she had spoken to Gladstone of her loss: he recorded how it 'continually returned upon her and met her at every turn — how in every thing great and small his [Albert's] ready, watchful mind, his taste, his affection, undertook all and effected all — for her business, her children, her very ornaments which all passed under the ordeal of his taste.' She told Gladstone that 'All this was gone from her, and the sun and light of her life was gone with it.' The Scottish views commemorate what Albert loved, what Albert left.

SEVEN

Family
and Empire

In 1887, when Queen Victoria celebrated her Golden Jubilee, the *Graphic* magazine was serializing Rider Haggard's classic empire adventure, *She*. Though Victoria's unrelenting weeds and sad widow's cap, the famous asperity of her tongue and the austerity of her household lessen the visual exoticism of her last decades, she herself was as much a part of the highly coloured romance of her times as Rider Haggard's imperishable heroine. When 'Fritz' Ponsonby, son of Victoria's private secretary, became an equerry at Court in the nineties, he was struck by the picture she presented at breakfast: 'Everything on the table was gold . . . and she was eating a boiled egg in a gold egg-cup with a gold spoon. Two Indian Khitmagars in scarlet and gold remained motionless behind her chair, while outside a page and a Scotchman in a kilt waited till she rang.' She was indeed the queen who held, in the words of Kipling's Jubilee hymn, 'dominion over palm and pine'.

Disraeli had made Victoria Empress of India in 1876, but only because she wanted it. The Commons and the Cabinet were against this change of the royal title, but the Queen, spellbound by its glamour, insisted. India was her last

Prince Alfred, Duke of Edinburgh, was in direct succession to the Dukedom of Saxe-Coburg-Gotha as well, and he had a house in the main square of Coburg, where his mother stayed in 1876. Luther had preached in the Moritzkirche, with its distinctive late Gothic spire, which also stood on the square.

195

In Greece water of Dragon formed, — in Northumper Dalmy Aug 9. 1882

enthusiasm in a lifetime of enthusiasms, and in this as in others she showed herself sovereign and impervious to criticism or dissent. In the case of John Brown, or of prolonged Highland visits, her tenacity was not so remarkable, for she was fighting a largely personal battle, but over India and the Indians she was uniquely free of the common prejudice prevalent all over England and in her own household. In 1857, when the Crown took over the government of India from the East India Company after the civil war and mutiny, the Queen and Prince Albert had tempered the proclamation with phrases much more tolerant and less imperialist than the original. She had objected to the document's missionary tone, for instance, and amended it to read: 'The deep attachment the Queen feels to her own religion and the comfort and happiness which she derives from its con-solations will preclude her from any attempt to interfere with the native religions . . . ' In the 1890s, having employed Indians as servants in her households at Osborne and Balmoral, she stopped her ears to the campaign of complaint raised by other members of the Court who, already disgruntled at the bands of Highland attendants, found

This watercolour of 1882, in which one can see the Queen's shakier grasp on her paintbrush, is one of the very few subjects she chose with an immediate political content. The Greece *was a troop ship transporting cavalry to Egypt, to support the Khedive against rebels who had been crushed by British intervention in June.*

196

Moslem customs as well too much to bear.

Victoria's attraction to the picturesque was deep-seated and instinctive, and she defended it against her attackers with loyal ferocity. In her youth the exotic settings of the ballet had seized her imagination; as early as 1833, she commented in fascination on the visit of a Captain Burnes, 'who had travelled over N.E. India' and brought 'some very interesting accounts' to Kensington Palace, as well as 'his servant, a native of Cabul, dressed in his native dress. He . . . is of a dark olive complexion and had a dress of real Cashmere made in the beautiful valley of Cashmere.' At a concert in the same year, she mentioned 'the oriental attire' of 'Prince Jame o deen, son of the famous Tippo Saib' (*sic*). But her account does not bristle with horror at the man whose father was a byword for cruelty; his life-size model of a carving of a tiger devouring an Englishman, complete with clockwork mechanical groans and moans, was found in his palace after its destruction and is now — perhaps inappropriately — in the Victoria and Albert Museum. In 1854 Victoria welcomed Dhuleep Singh, son of the Chief of the Sikhs, who had been removed from his throne as a child by the British. When she learned that the boy was showing no sympathy with British victims of the mutiny and its aftermath, the Queen defended him, pointing out that he was hardly in a position to delight in British victories, 'or be expected to *like* to hear his country-people called *fiends* and *monsters*, and to see them brought in hundreds, if not thousands, to be executed' and ending, 'It is a great mercy that he, poor boy, is not there.' She was convinced of his Eastern gentleness and touched by his 'striking good looks'; she painted him in watercolour at Osborne as, covered in jewels, he played with her children.

To be Empress of these beautiful, dazzling creatures was pure romance. At the reception of the Indian deputations for the Golden Jubilee Victoria retrieved from her past stock of images a word she had hardly used since the happy days of her marriage: the Princes' appearance was 'like a dream'. They had 'wonderful jewels on'; they lavished magnificent gifts on her; Sir Partab Singh placed his sword at her feet, and

told her everything he possessed was hers to use. After the Colonial and Indian Exhibition, forty-three Indian craftsmen paraded before Victoria and 'knelt down and kissed and stroked my feet and knees, some prostrating themselves more than others.' The Empress of India was not displeased.

She would like to have seen for herself her sub-continent, and her remarks to Vicky during the Prince of Wales's resplendent tour of 1876 have a touch of jealousy to them: 'Bertie's progresses lose a little interest and are very wearing — as there is such a constant repetition of elephants — trappings — jewels — illuminations and fireworks.' But if she could not experience India in person, she would create the atmosphere of the civilized, paternalist Orient at home; she would bring, incongruous as it may seem, the majesty of the Raj to the homely Isle of Wight.

The Queen's first two Indian servants, whose photographs still hang in her dressing room just beneath one of John Brown and his brothers, were Mohammed Buxsh and Abdul Karim. They entered her service three days after the Golden Jubilee. The former was large, bearded and genial, but little else is known of him, for he never climbed higher than the

199

rank of bearer. But the latter became more loathed even than John Brown. On the day they kissed her feet and began to wait on her at Windsor, the Queen wrote that Abdul Karim was 'much younger [he was twenty-four], much lighter, tall, and with a fine serious countenance.' She knew that the father of the Munshi ('Teacher') was a native doctor in Agra. Her courtiers, suspicious that the Munshi was working for his own Moslem ends and endangering the Queen's impartiality in the agonising religious problems of India, worked to discredit him. When they found that his father was only a hospital attendant in the Indian medical department, they pounced. But Abdul was clever and quick-witted and charming, and the Queen cried fiddlesticks at her household, issued terse reprimands about 'red-tapist' narrowminded-ness, and thought the inlaid marble chess table sent to her by Abdul's father worthy of a place at Osborne beside the famous Renaissance-style billiard table Albert himself had designed, and a painted *guéridon* from the Vatican.

Shortly after the Munshi's arrival, the Queen recorded in her journal: 'Am learning a few words of Hindustani to speak to my servants. It is a great interest to me, for both the language and the people.' The Munshi soon explained to the Queen that waiting was beneath him, since at home he had been a clerk. Photographs in which he appeared as a menial were speedily destroyed, and his advancement began. Before the eyes of attendants who could hardly bring themselves to speak to an Indian, the Munshi was given Karim Cottage at Balmoral, Frogmore Cottage at Windsor, and Arthur Cottage at Osborne. Despatch boxes about Indian affairs were shown to him, his advice was solicited, and he was taking part in the holy privacy of family theatricals, as a figure in the 'tableau vivant' of an Indian bazaar.

The last full-scale paintings Victoria attempted are copies of portraits, one of the Munshi in 1889, the other of Mohammed Burhsh in 1892. The originals were painted by Rudolph Swoboda, a Viennese and the nephew of L. K. Müller, who was not only gifted at exotic foreign genre scenes but also won high favour as a portrait painter to the aristocracy. Swoboda was the last artist to receive full patronage from the Queen. He came to London via Egypt, where he had specialized in bazaar vignettes. The Queen chose him to be her eyes on India, commissioning him first to paint the craftsmen at the Colonial Exhibition, and then sending him on a journey to India itself to record for her the typical features of her new subjects, their everyday life and activities.

Swoboda's enormous collection of small oil sketches, vivid, colourful and wrongly neglected, hangs in the Indian Corridor at Osborne, alongside portraits of Indian loyalists such as Sir Partab Singh and Maharajah Dhuleep Singh by Winterhalter. The Corridor leads to the largest building undertaken by Victoria after Albert's death, and, in its flash display — just as the bleak bothy of Glassalt Shiel is in its humility — it is entirely characteristic of the Queen who had loved dressing up as a child. The Durbar Room occupies a whole wing, opposite the earlier Household Wing at Osborne. It is an enormous, single reception room, lit by tall, rather un-Indian, sash windows overlooking the lawn, and decorated throughout in the elaborate plasterwork of peacocks, rosettes, arabesques and scrolls characteristic of Mudejar work in Spain. It was designed by John Lockwood Kipling, father of Rudyard and keeper of the museum at Lahore, with the help of a master of Indian stucco technique, Bhai Ram Singh, and it was used throughout the nineties as a banqueting hall in which the Empress of India and the 'Mother of Europe', a tiny, stout, dazzling figure, would appear, laden with the enormous gems and cabochons presented to her by the subjects of the Raj.

By 1897 and the Diamond Jubilee, the Queen and Empress was a living icon. In New Guinea, some of the most distant tribes under British rule failed to make the distinction between monarchy and divinity, and worshipped the Queen as their holy Mother. Photogravure had made her face familiar to everyone: her famous profile, of which even the sloping chin cannot efface the determination, was discerned in the silhouettes of American mountains; her bell-like figure,

Osborne
July – 1860 –

Little Charlotte of Prussia (our
granddaughter.)

stiff in its mourning crape and surmounted by her widow's cap (which she would not even put off for the Jubilee processions), became in the eyes of the world the image of the archetypal mother.

Family trees, with medallions of her progeny hanging like fruit from the branches, were published in newspapers and magazines all over the Empire for her Jubilees. Victoria was the sturdiest vine the English royal house had ever known. By 1879 she was already a great-grandmother: Vicky's eldest daughter, Charlotte of Prussia, gave birth to a girl, Princess Feodora of Saxe Meiningen. 'Quite an event', commented the sixty-year old Queen. Victoria's children were vigorously fertile: Vicky bore eight children in all, in fourteen years — two died in childhood; Alice had seven children in eleven years, lost one aged three, and, while nursing her last-born, 'May', caught diphtheria and died in 1878, by some freak of destiny on the same day — 'the terrible day come round again' — as her father, 14 December. She was buried at Darmstadt, the home of her marriage, but her effigy, with May in her arms, carved in marble by Boehm, lies in the mausoleum at Frogmore beside her father.

All the children's birthdays, and all the children's children's birthdays, were remembered by the Queen with a card; even her fortune could not extend to gifts for the fifty or so offspring. When Alice died, she visited her Hesse home and took special care of the orphans, including red-haired Alix. In 1894, when Alix married the Tsar, the Queen wrote wonderingly: 'How I thought of darling Alicky, and how impossible it seemed that that gentle little simple Alicky should be the great Empress of Russia.' But Victoria began to lose interest as the numbers grew. To Vicky, on the birth of Margaret in 1872, she expressed her weariness: 'I don't dislike babies, though I find very young ones rather disgusting, and I take interest in those of my children when there are two or three ... But when they come at the rate of three a year it becomes a cause of mere anxiety for my own children and of not great interest. What name is this fourth daughter to have?'

The Princess of Wales bore Bertie five children in five years, but the last baby died at birth; Alfred's wife Marie, Grand Duchess of Russia, had five children; Lenchen, who became Princess Christian of Schleswig-Holstein, had five; Louise of Prussia, Arthur's wife, had a modest three; Beatrice, before her husband Henry of Battenberg died of fever in 1896 on the Ashanti expedition, had four; only Louise, Duchess of Argyll, had none. Leopold, when he died in 1884, left two children, of whom the young Princess Alice, Countess of Athlone, is still alive. Victoria's father, the Duke of Kent, had been born in 1767. Four generations only, in two hundred odd years: the span is astonishing.

Victoria became the ancestor of kings and queens, and emperors and empresses in the last throw of dynastic optimism in Europe. Her grandchildren before the upheaval of the First World War sat on the thrones of Russia, Norway, Spain, Germany, Greece, Roumania and Great Britain. Through the Coburgs, her descendants ruled in Belgium and Portugal. Of these only the thrones of Elizabeth II, Baudouin I, Olav V of Norway, Gustav VI of Sweden and the restored Juan Carlos of Spain have survived. The addresses of other descendants bear witness to their widespread dispossession and exile: they live in apartments in Lausanne and Rome and Madrid. But Victoria's pencil, in the seventies and eighties, knew nothing of their future glory or their future diminution. When children were gathered around her for holidays in Scotland or the Isle of Wight, she still delighted in their merriment and play. 'Baby' Margaret, eldest daughter of the favourite son Arthur, had 'her likeness' drawn when she visited her grandmother at Balmoral in the first year of her life. The many different 'Babies' who processed through the drawing rooms of Balmoral and Osborne before their awesome but ever indulgent 'Gangan' were committed to paper, often on sheets banded with mourning black. The Queen still favoured back views and details of big bows and sashes. She usually ignored the adults, especially if the visit were formal, like her grandson the Kaiser's ostentatiously grand descents on Osborne.

Above: One of Victoria's chief preoccupations after Albert's death was to find her eldest son, Bertie, the future King, a suitable bride. The lovely Princess Alexandra of Denmark was suggested by Vicky; the Queen was won over completely by the gentleness and charm of 'Alix', and made this profile drawing of her.

Right: On a sheet of writing paper heavily bordered in black, 'Gangan', then aged sixty-nine, drew the flounces and bow on her granddaughter Margaret, eldest child of Arthur, Duke of Connaught.

Her eyesight was dimming and her hand was shakier, but she still drew with pleasure. As in the early years of mourning, people occupied her less than scenery. The final sketchpads record mostly the views from the villas in which she stayed on her last years' annual holidays abroad, and, as always, scenes from the windows of the railway carriage. Queen Victoria's curiosity and gaiety did not diminish with age (the principal reason we have for thinking her severe and mirthless is that photographs in the eighties and nineties had to be exposed too long to capture a smile): excursions were still a source of delight, and she became more adventurous as she grew older, visiting Switzerland for the first time in 1868, Italy in 1879, the South of France in 1882, Spain in 1889. Her travelling style reflects her roots in the eighteenth century and its traditions of the Grand Tour. She was almost always incognito. In 1868 in Switzerland she was known as the Countess of Kent; in 1879 in Italy as the Countess of Balmoral. But the magnificent special trains, the immense suites, entire hotels and great villas made over to accommodate them did not disguise her for long. Yet in the midst of her extravagant ways, the girlish gush of pleasure at new

This impression of the built-up skyline looking towards Whitehall was painted by Victoria from the Little Pavilion, designed by Prince Albert

In the last decades of her painting life, the seventies and eighties, Queen Victoria's eyesight was weakening, but she was still sensitive to transformations in the light, colour and atmosphere of familiar and much painted places, like Loch Callater and the harbour fort of Cherbourg.

sights and new experiences remained. An ostrich egg omelette given to her by a dubious French countess at Cimiez in 1899 prompted the question: 'Why cannot we have ostrich eggs at Windsor? We *have* an ostrich.' 'Yes, mama', replied Princess Beatrice. 'A male one.' In the South of France, Sarah Bernhardt was invited to perform before her; in Switzerland she visited the birthplace of William Tell, hero of the opera in which, so many years before, she had loved to watch the dance of La Tyrolienne.

Up to 1890, she was still busy painting throughout her holidays, seeking out splendid views with the help of local guides, sometimes ambitiously covering a double sheet with an Alpine range 'glowing in the setting sun, what is called here "Alpenglühen". It was glorious . . . ' After 1890, her eyesight worsened, and her aides were commanded to write larger and larger in blacker and blacker ink on paper so thick that it could not be folded into the despatch boxes.

The last sketchbook of her life is dated 1885–88. It contains a tentative portrait of one of the dogs who always kept her company; the trembling outline of poplars, turning gold in autumn, and the blue haze lying over the view from her window at Aix-les-Bains; the crest of Mont Blanc, 'seen from the railway'; and, last of all, a skilful quick drawing of her Indian cavalry, turbanned and carrying banners. With the exception of the second Baby Beatrice, youngest daughter of Alfred, whom the Queen sketched in June 1890 when she was six, these Sikh horsemen fittingly provided the last, admiring image from the pen of their Empress.

Epilogue

In an undated memorandum, written towards the end of her life, the Queen listed her sketchbooks and the albums of paintings and photographs in her collection and left them 'to be considered heirlooms of the Crown'. She included Albert's drawings, commissioned views of places she had visited and houses she had lived in, and her own work: the portraits of the children as well as 'all my sketchbooks from nature'. She prized them; she did not make great claims for her talents, but she believed in good husbandry in all things, and she knew that her gifts, in art as in music as in letters, had been nurtured with care and fruitfulness. She was much more vain about her writing than her painting, amusing her courtiers with a sudden literary turn in her conversation after the publication of *Leaves*. But her regard for her albums was justified. She for whom preservation was a sacred duty, preserved in her sketches the fugitive images of her life and character, of her curiosity and her affections, her immediacy and gusto, her extraordinary simplicity in the midst of grandeur, her private values, so well defended in the course of the greatest public office and the closest public scrutiny. She stands in the centre of her accessible, coherent world, responding, not projecting, dissolving the formal barriers of majesty so that what she puts down on paper is not the pomp but the pastimes — not the relation of hierarchy, but of intimacy. She is never profound, but because she is always personal, she is not trivial either, always alert to the straightforward quiddity of her subjects: mountains are grand, the sea in summer is blue, the flounces on her children's petticoats are gay. The same absence of obliqueness that made her peremptory and sometimes wrong-headed as a queen, that led her to declare her likes and her dislikes so imperiously, gives her assurance and freshness as a draughtsman.

Her art is an exclamation at life, like the punctuation in her journal and the underlinings in her letters; through it we see her round eyes widen, her small mouth part, her brow wrinkle at the effort to take down the images as they passed by all too quickly in a life in which increasingly it seemed that she was the only fixed star while so many others fell, as the shooting stars she had watched with Albert on the balcony at Osborne had fallen into the sea. Her painting commands us to participate in her uncomplicated vitality — though the gift for enjoyment, when possessed as fully as she possessed it, is no uncomplicated thing.

Without apology, without irony, without hyperbole, she took down life's pleasures as they had been granted to her in abundance, and disregarded majesty and state; few crowns, few sceptres, or obeisances of subjects, few moments of high seriousness or glory solemnize her pages. Little William urges on the toy coach from the box; William, Emperor of Prussia, is absent. The crystal vault of the Great Exhibition is not here, but the pure regularity of Albert's face at twenty. Her Indian dominions pass unmentioned, except for the soft olive sheen of Abdul Karim's cheek. The battles, imperial and splendid, fought during her reign are missing, but Arthur and Alfred, soldier and sailor, do duty in fancy dress. Lord M. is there, unruly hair and blue-grey eyes, with Islay playing on his

Little William of Prussia gave his grandmother warning of his mettle early on. She wrote that her daughter Beatrice was 'rather afraid' of him 'as he is so violent', and she caught his determination in this drawing of William playing coachman to his sister Charlotte.

knees; the political changes and reforms of the century inspire not a brushstroke. Heather dyes the mountain slopes mauve and grey and emerald. Broom turns golden at Balmoral and zinnias flame on the terraces at Osborne; Albert's Rosenau stands white amongst the trees; the tribe plays on the lawn. The stags fall under Albert's gun; Baby has stiff red hair and Daisy's bow is well puffed up; Annie MacDonald draws her plaid over her head; Bertie is in armour for the play; the poor ex–Duke of Brunswick has dangerous dark eyes; Grisi wrings her tragic hands; Lehzen looks coolly down her nose; the gipsies are outside with bundles of kindling; the horses of her girlhood break into a gallop; and on stage Taglioni is dancing with a smile.

Bibliography

Principal Sources

Queen Victoria's Sketchbooks at Windsor Castle.
Queen Victoria's Sketchbook belonging to H.R.H. The Duke of Kent.
Queen Victoria's Journal, in the Royal Archives (referred to in References as RA QVJ).

Victoria, Queen,   *Dearest Child, Private Correspondence of Queen Victoria and the Princess Royal, 1858–61*, edited by Roger Fulford (London, 1964). (Referred to as *Dearest Child*.)
Darling Child, Letters between Queen Victoria and the Crown Princess of Prussia, 1871–78, edited by Roger Fulford (London, 1976). (Referred to as *Darling Child*.)
The Girlhood of Queen Victoria, A Selection from Her Majesty's Diaries between the Years 1832 and 1840, edited by Viscount Esher, 3 vols. (London, 1907). (Referred to as *Girlhood*.)
Leaves from a Journal. With introduction by Raymond Mortimer (London, 1961). (Referred to as *Leaves 1855*.)
Leaves from the Journal of Our Life in the Highlands from 1848 to 1861, edited by Arthur Helps (London, 1868). (Referred to as *Leaves*.)
More Leaves from the Journal of a Life in the Highlands (London, 1884). (Referred to as *More Leaves*.)
The Letters of Queen Victoria, A Selection from Her Majesty's Correspondence, First Series, 1837–61, edited by A.C. Benson and Viscount Esher, 3 vols. (London, 1907). Second Series, 1862–85, edited by G.E. Buckle, 3 vols (London, 1926). Third Series, 1886–1901, edited by G.E. Buckle, 3 vols. (London, 1930). (Referred to as *Letters*.)

Select Bibliography

Ames, Winslow, *Prince Albert and the Victorian Taste* (London, 1967).
Bennett, Daphne, *King without a Crown: Albert, Prince Consort of England 1819–61* (London, 1977).

Fulford, Roger, *Hanover to Windsor* (London, 1960).

Hobhouse, Hermione, *Thomas Cubitt, Master Builder* (London, 1971).

Lehmann, John, *Edward Lear and His World* (London, 1977).

Lennie, Campbell, *Landseer, the Victorian Paragon* (London, 1976).

Longford, Elizabeth, *Victoria R.I.* (London, 1964).

MacGeorge, A., *W.L. Leitch, Landscape Painter: A Memoir* (London, 1884).

Mallet, Victor (ed.), *Life with Queen Victoria: Marie Mallet's Letters from Court 1887–1901* (London, 1968).

Matson, John, *Dear Osborne* (London, 1978).

Ponsonby, Sir Frederick, *Recollections of Three Reigns* (London, date not known).

Rowell, George, *Queen Victoria Goes to the Theatre* (London, 1978).

Scheele, Godfrey and Margaret, *The Prince Consort* (London, 1977).

Strachey, Lytton, *Queen Victoria* (London, reprinted 1971).

Wood, Christopher, *A Dictionary of Victorian Painters* (London, 1972).

Woodham-Smith, Cecil, *Queen Victoria: Her Life and Times*, vol. i, 1819–61 (London, 1972).

Young, G.M., *Portrait of an Age: Victorian England* (Oxford, reprinted 1973).

References

See bibliography for full titles of sources.

Chapter 1

p.11	Not fond of learning	*Letters*, I, vol. i, p.15
p.13	Fanny Kemble	RA QVJ 20 Aug 1835
p.13	Elizabeth I's Latin	RA QVJ 8 Nov 1832
p.14	Daily routine	RA QVJ 9 Feb 1833
p.14	Westall's praise	RA QVJ 19 Nov 1832
p.14	Westall's work	RA QVJ 4 Nov 1832
p.17	Westall's death	RA QVJ 6 Dec 1836
p.20	Westall's penury	RA QVJ 13 Dec 1836
p.23	Unhappiness	*Dearest Child*, 9 June 1858
p.24	Feodore's unhappiness	*Letters* I, i, p.24
p.26	Feodore's charm	*Letters* I, i, p.17
p.26	Eliza's departure	RA QVJ 25–6 July 1834
p.27	Eliza's character	RA QVJ 2 Mar 1851
p.28	Victoire stays	RA QVJ 23 Dec 1832
p.28	Victoire dines	RA QVJ 16 Dec 1832
p.28	Victoire rides	RA QVJ 17 May 1832
p.31	Victoria's progresses	RA QVJ 13 Oct 1832
p.36	How Queens ought to be	*Letters* I, i, 19 Nov 1834
p.36	Other Queens	RA QVJ 16 Sep 1833
p.37	Donna Maria's education	*Letters* I, i, p.76
p.39	Widows at St Leonards	RA QVJ 7 Jan 1835
p.45	Gipsies wronged	RA QVJ 5 Jan 1837

Chapter 2

p.51	La Sylphide doll	RA QVJ 18 Aug 1832
p.51	Taglioni flying	RA QVJ 5 June 1834
p.51	Taglioni fawn-like	RA QVJ 2 June 1835
p.51	Taglioni sylph-like	RA QVJ 27 June 1835
p.52	Thackeray and Taglioni	18 July 1829: *Letters and Private Papers of W.M. Thackeray*, ed. G.N. Ray, vol i (Oxford, 1945)
p.52	Victoria as Taglioni	RA QVJ 6 Jan 1833
p.54	Revolt of the Naiades	RA QVJ 24 Jan 1834
p.55	The 'Unknown' man	RA QVJ 9 Mar 1832
p.57	Melbourne and actresses	RA QVJ 2 Jan 1839
p.59	Cooper in *The King's Seal*	RA QVJ 19 Mar 1835
p.60	*The Miller and His Men*	RA QVJ 18 Feb 1835
p.63	Albert likes the music	RA QVJ 17 July 1845
p.63	Terpsichorean feelings	*Letters* I, i, pp.78–9
p.63	Prefers opera to ballet	RA QVJ 2 June 1835
p.66	Prefers Grisi to Malibran	RA QVJ 18 May 1835
p.68	Grisi in person	RA QVJ 11 May 1835
p.68	Grisi as Elena	RA QVJ 14 May 1835
p.69	Grisi at her birthday concert	RA QVJ 18 May 1835
p.69	White roses like Grisi	RA QVJ 11 Sep 1835
p.71	Lablache in *Prova di una Opera Seria*	RA QVJ 2 June 1835
p.72	Lablache's lessons	RA QVJ 28 June 1836
p.72	Mozart	RA QVJ 18 Apr 1837
p.75	Grisi's fear of failing	RA QVJ 18 Apr 1837
p.75	Victoria quite cross	RA QVJ 6 June 1837

Chapter 3

p.78	Victoria alone	RA QVJ 20 June 1837
p.80	Her height	RA QVJ 23 Feb 1838
p.80	Her fine character	RA QVJ 12 Feb 1838
p.80	Confidence in Melbourne	RA QVJ 9 Jan 1838
p.81	Fear of losing Melbourne	RA QVJ 8 May 1839; *Letters* I, i, pp.200–201

Chapter 7

Index

References to illustration captions are in italics. V.=Queen Victoria; A.=Prince Albert.